The Need For
SPIRITUAL
COMMUNITIES
and How To Start Them

The Need For
SPIRITUAL
COMMUNITIES
and How To Start Them

Swami Kriyananda

Crystal Clarity Publishers
Nevada City, California

Crystal Clarity Publishers, Nevada City, CA 95959

First printing 1968
Second edition, revised and updated, 1988
Third edition, revised and updated, 2013

Printed in the United States of America

ISBN-13: 978-1-56589-294-1
ePub ISBN-13: 978-1-56589-555-3

Front cover photo and design by Nirmala Starner Schuppe
Back cover and interior design by David Jensen

[CIP data block available]

⊕ crystal clarity **publishers**
www.crystalclarity.com
clarity@crystalclarity.com
800-424-1055

PUBLISHER'S NOTE

Some readers might be interested to know the genesis of this book, which has taken a few twists and turns over the years. Swami Kriyananda originally wrote this work before he founded his first community, Ananda Village, in order to interest people in the project. Part I, which presents Kriyananda's essential concepts about communities, was first published in 1968, under the title *Cooperative Communities: How to Start Them and Why*. In 1971 the author republished the book with the addition of Part II about the development of Ananda, and how those developments might offer insights to those wishing to found communities of their own. He updated the book further in 1979.

In 1988 he revised Part I of that book and published it (without Part II) under the title *Intentional Communities*. Now, for this 2013 edition, he naturally used that 1988 rewrite in place of the 1979 version. And in addition he edited the entire book once more, but with an eye to keeping each Part's voice back in the time when it was originally written.

He also added a new (second) Afterword, written from his current standpoint in April of 2013. It proved to be the last of his published writings, completed not three weeks before his passing.

PREFACE

I first wrote and published this little book in 1968. My purpose at that time was twofold: to suggest general guidelines for people interested in communities; and to offer a blueprint for an intentional community that I myself wanted to found. My hope was to enlist a number of friends in this venture.

Nearly thirty years of research went into the writing of this handbook. My thrust, during that preparatory period, was never romantic or academic. It was always to provide workable guidelines. I enjoyed reading "utopian" novels about idyllic societies, as much, probably, as anyone. My concern, however, was never with beautiful but impractical theories. It was with concepts that stood a chance of being actually realized on the hard ground of this world.

I first became interested in cooperative communities when I was fifteen. World War II was raging at that time. America, following the disaster of Pearl Harbor, had just entered the conflict. Perhaps it was the hatred and suffering generated by war that helped push me in the direction of seeking an alternative to the arrogant self-affirmation and selfish nationalism that was the spur to that conflict. To me, even then, the thought of people of basically similar interests living in community, and sharing together the struggles of life, offered the best possible answer to some of the pressing problems of our times.

For many years thereafter I fairly devoured every book I could find on communities, past and present. Whenever I could, I visited functioning communities. One such was Dayalbagh, near Agra in India. Another was a kibbutz, near Galilee in Israel. I also visited and studied, from a communitarian point of view, numerous monastic communities throughout the world.

I spoke and corresponded, as well, with a number of people whose expertise might offer solutions to some of the practical problems I anticipated in the founding of a workable community. Among these people was Jayprakash Narayan, formerly the number two man in India after Jawaharlal Nehru. Jayprakash Narayan had left government service in the hope of finding communitarian solutions to India's problems. He was gracious enough to express enthusiasm for my ideas.

My adult work as an organizer, administrator, teacher, and counselor provided me with direct, practical experience in the intricacies of group dynamics.

Most valuable of all to me were years that I spent meditating on the question of why some communities succeeded, and others failed. Especially I sought to attune myself to inner, divine guidance, for no project can succeed greatly without some guidance from above, which is to say, from the superconscious.

My enthusiasm for this project received added impetus when, in 1948, I met the great master Paramhansa Yogananda, and was accepted by him as a disciple. For I soon learned that the communitarian ideal was dear to him also.

One of the basic aims of Yogananda's mission to the West was thus stated by him: "To spread a spirit of brotherhood among all peoples, and to aid in establishing, in many countries, self-sustaining world brotherhood colonies for plain living and high thinking."

For years, as his disciple, I studied everything he had said to me and others, and everything he had written, on this subject. I also devoted long meditative effort to attuning myself inwardly to his thoughts, for a person's concepts can be understood in their true essence only *from within.*

Shortly after completing this book, I founded Ananda[1] Co-operative Village in the Sierra Nevada foothills of Northern California. That was in 1968. Since then, our communities have become recognized as one of the most successful network of "New Age" communities in the world.

The present book, too, like Ananda, has gained widespread recognition as a guidebook to the founding of successful communities.

The second part of this volume, written in 1971, presents the story, often dramatic, of Ananda's founding. In 1979, a section was added to bring the reader up to date on subsequent developments.

My sense of the importance of cooperative communities has not diminished over the years. It has only grown. The

---

1 "Ananda" is a Sanskrit word that means "divine inner joy." —ed.

Chapter One
THE TIME IS NOW

In his last years on earth, the great teacher, Paramhansa Yogananda, repeatedly and urgently spoke of a plan that he said was destined to become a basic social pattern for the new age: the formation of Self-realization cooperative communities, or "world brotherhood colonies." In almost every public lecture, no matter what his announced topic, he would digress to urge people to act upon this proposal.

"The day will come," he predicted, "when this idea will spread through the world like wildfire. Gather together, those of you who share high ideals. Pool your resources. Buy land in the country. A simple life will bring you inner freedom. Harmony with nature will bring you a happiness known to few city dwellers. In the company of other truth seekers you will find it easier to meditate and to think of God.

"What is the need for all the luxury with which people surround themselves? Most of what they have they are paying for on the installment plan! Their debts are a source of unending worry to them. Even people whose luxuries have been paid for have no freedom. Attachment makes them slaves. They consider themselves freer for possessing possessions, but don't see that their possessions in turn have possessed them!"

Yogananda stressed the joys of simple, Godly thinking and natural living—a way of life that, he said, would bring people "happiness and freedom." But his message went beyond simply presenting people with an attractive idea. There was an urgency in his plea.

"The time is short," he repeatedly told his audiences. "You have no idea of the sufferings that await mankind. In addition to wars, there will be a depression the like of which has not been known in a very long time. Money will not be worth the paper it is printed on. Millions will die [presumably through war and starvation]."

Once he declared fervently, "You don't know what a terrible cataclysm is coming!"

To rely on prophetic utterances may strike some people as superstitious. Even those who view them as such, however, may be interested to note that, of persons reputed to have prophetic vision, every single one has predicted terrible sufferings for humanity in the years to come. It is not necessary, however, to rely blindly on prophecy. The turmoil they predict is already too visibly probable.

Numerous biologists have stated with absolute finality that the present population explosion can have only one result: In the near future "hundreds of millions" of people in the world must either die of starvation for lack of sufficient food on our planet to feed them, or be destroyed in a nuclear holocaust as they struggle for whatever food they can get. Economic depression of massive proportions has been predicted by reputable economists. And as for warfare, one must, of course, always hope for the best—but what real chances are there, think you, for a cessation of conflict? The pressures continue to mount. They have not lessened even the threat of global destruction. If only one atom bomb is dropped, can you imagine that there won't be retaliation?

Let us consider the solution that Yogananda proposed— that of Self-realization cooperatives, or "world brotherhood colonies." It was, to be sure, a personal, not a universal solution that he stressed. Yet many universal changes have proceeded from personal transformations. (Witness the widespread up-liftment that grew out of the teachings of Buddha and of Jesus Christ. The ensuing social revolutions were out of all propor-tion to the few disciples converted by those great masters.)

There is, moreover, at this time in history, an implication in this idea of communal cooperatives that lifts it quite out of the personal category into something sociological and universal.

Chapter Two
SELF-REALIZATION VS. THE MEGALOPOLIS

No sociologist is needed to convince one that the trend of these last two centuries has been toward consolidation. Small businesses, unable to compete with the large corporations, have become swallowed up by them. Large corporations, again, have merged with others, in time becoming vast industrial empires.

Societies of men are moving inexorably toward a centralization of power. The world's increasing population necessitates increasing governmental control. The old argument between states' rights and federal rights is an anachronism. It is impossible nowadays, legislatively and economically, to return the power to local governments. The trend, instead, has been toward a consolidation not only of cities and states, but of countries.

For man, the individual, what will be the result of all this consolidation?

It is in the interest of economy and efficiency that groups of people unite. The danger is that those same principles— economy and efficiency—will demand of people a uniformity that extends to their personal lives as well. Numerous social thinkers have noted that individual tastes and values, too, must be, and *are* being, increasingly subordinated to the institutional order—the "Establishment."

To institutional minds, such uniformity may seem in itself an end—even a blessing. Such people decry individualism as selfish. Indeed, if individualism is centered in the ego, rather than in personal integrity, it is wrong. "Group think," however, if looked upon as the only alternative to selfishness, is a descent into mindlessness. If anyone supporting such a trend is hailed as a "liberal," conscience itself becomes "pack consciousness."

Is it truly liberal to *destroy* liberty? Voluntary cooperation is one thing, but enforced conformity, quite another. The hammer and sickle of communism is a mockery. Even the animals place a priority on intelligence. Witness a small pack of dogs. Always, the leader is not the largest and strongest. It may be only a little dog, but always it will be the brightest one. The ruling communists in Russia eliminated the intellectuals, not because they despised them, but because they considered them the supreme threat to their leadership. Indeed, communism has been the last gasp of materialistic atheism before a growth in more spiritual awareness. It is a materialistic religion—the last stand before the increasing spiritual awareness in this new age of energy.

There is a third alternative before us. *It lies in a recognition of the fact that the mainspring of mature action is always the inner man, not the outer social order he lives in.*

To imagine that systems can be anything more than a convenience has been man's mistake. Systems are not an end in themselves. They cannot inspire men to perfection. At best, they may prevent a few people from behaving too outrageously.

The more society becomes centralized in its power, the greater the need for individuals to seek their values (as opposed to their outer convenience) *within themselves*. For man is more than a cog in the social wheel. The systems he adopts are supposed in some way to benefit *him*, individually, and not merely to serve the good of some separate entity, unrelated to any of its members, called "society." To speak of society, as some writers have done, as an "organism," is misleading. From *within* ourselves come our inspiration, our understanding, our love and happiness. All that we experience outside ourselves depends upon our inner *capacity* for experience. Man is a *source* of light, not a mirror.

Thus, the point must come in modern social evolution when men, instead of succumbing passively to outward demands for uniformity, rise up individually to reassert their dignity as human beings.

The trend of which we speak is inevitable. In fact, it has already begun. Offsetting the push to uniformity, in fact, the modern era has seen a rising tide of insistence on the dignity of the individual. In communistic countries the governments have tried to curb this tendency, yet even there it is clearly in evidence.

It was even in evidence in the utterly dehumanizing atmosphere of the World War II concentration camps. Even there, individuals could be found who, in personal resistance to the sordid influences around them, rose like lotuses from the mud and blossomed into greatness.

It is time to press forward from a preoccupation with outward systems to a recognition of the real key to the efficacy of any system: individual man. The need of the hour has come for self-unfoldment—not as a selfish imposition on the universe (the "Great God, EGO" of Ayn Rand)—but simply as a private and deeply personal search for Self-realization.

The result cannot but benefit man in his political, economic, and social institutions as well. For all things bring harmony to men who have found harmony in themselves. And nothing brings it to those in whom inner discord prevails.

The question arises: How, without imposing on anyone else, may one develop inner clarity in the midst of social confusion? It is difficult to have inner peace when one is surrounded by chaos. It is difficult to progress steadily in one direction through swirling currents that seek to draw one off in a million other directions.

Consider: What real need is there to cling to city life? If it doesn't happen to suit one, what moral end can be served by sticking grimly to it? The chance that it may somehow become molded in time to become a universal blessing? It is not his systems that bless man, but man who blesses his systems by having the good will to make them work.

No, it is not necessary from any standpoint—social, philosophical, personal—to remain in an environment that is not conducive to one's welfare. For the man of aspiring mind, the megalopolis of modern times ceases to be even the convenience that so many people find it. Instead, it becomes an obstruction.

He must find his way, just as soon as circumstances allow him to do so, to the sanity and peace of a simpler way of life.

A person who devotes himself to the development of an inner awareness is in a vastly better position than one who, his very self-respect assaulted by competing hordes, has all he can do to maintain a little sense of his own identity.

One reads with horror newspaper accounts of people who watched calmly, refusing to become involved, as some major crime was committed, or as someone fell and died in the street. It would seem that the average city dweller's technique for preserving his sanity is to isolate himself from the world around him, and from his fellow man. Stranded and alone on the tiny island of his ego, is it any wonder that he complains of feeling alienated?

"This above all," Shakespeare wrote, "to thine own self be true, and it must follow, as the night the day, thou canst not then be false to any man."

Without self-respect, how can there be a proper respect for others? Without self-awareness, how can there be a sensitivity to their needs? The wellsprings of charity must flow from the inner man. They cannot reach him by a process of invasion.

To "hie away" to the country, then, need in no way imply a rejection of one's social responsibilities. It can become, rather, the beginning of a sincere assumption of responsibility, not only for oneself, but, by extension, toward society at large.

Chapter Three
INTENTIONAL COMMUNITIES AND
THE QUEST FOR OPPORTUNITY

Why do people move to the city? The main reasons are easy to find. In cities, jobs are more plentiful, social life is more varied, cultural stimuli are incomparably greater than in rural areas. There is a statement in the Hindu scriptures: "For the peaceless, how is happiness possible?" Thoughts are actual things. People influence one another with the calmness or restlessness of their thoughts; with the nobility or baseness of their mental attitudes; with the loftiness or crudeness of their aspirations. In cities, one lives constantly exposed to the uplifting and debasing influences around him.

I have had many opportunities to experience the truth of these statements. Some years ago, I lived in San Francisco near a busy thoroughfare. My apartment, however, was enough separated from that highway for me only barely to hear the traffic. I often noticed, if I happened to wake up at, say, three o'clock in the morning, that there was much more peace in the atmosphere around me than during the busy hours. It wasn't so much the reduction of sound as the fact that everyone around me was asleep.

On one occasion I had to go into the nightclub district of that city. Prior to going, I made it a point to chant a spiritual song and melody. Armed with this inner peace, I set out into that area. It was amazing to me to note how the thought forms around me were as if reaching out to me, trying to clutch at me with the invitation, "Come in!" I had no interest whatever in accepting that thought. Nevertheless, I could feel it as something real.

I suppose years of meditation had made me more sensitive to those thought forms. Even so, the influences there exert a powerful effect.

In 1958 I went from Bangkok to Cambodia to see Angkor Wat. I was struck there by the feeling that a dark, heavy cloud hung over that country. Not much later the whole world was shocked by the political tragedy that occurred there. I have experienced a similar, though less dense, cloud over Germany. Over England I have felt not a cloud so much as a chill, a lack of heart feeling; I do not care to go there, even though my happiest school years were spent there, before the war. In America I feel kindness and generosity, but also an unpleasant sense of self-importance. My Guru once said to me, "England is finished." When I tried to temper that statement, he merely waved a hand dismissively and repeated, "Finished! Finished!" Of Europe, he said, "Europe will be devastated; Russia, annihilated." I myself have always felt that Italy, with its many saints, has greater devotion to God than most countries. Love of God is the greatest protection.

When America dropped two atom bombs over Japan, one over Hiroshima and the other over Nagasaki, I have read that two religious communities, a Franciscan and a Jesuit, even though they were located near the epicenter of those cataclysmic events, were nevertheless kept untouched.

People's consciousness exerts the strongest influence, but consciousness is everywhere—even in the stones.[2*]

Deserts, especially, have a purifying influence. The sound of AUM there is powerful and soothing. Yogananda said of the desert area around Twentynine Palms, California, "This is the Kingdom of AUM!"

I live in California. It has often amazed me, when entering that state from Nevada, Oregon, or Mexico, how the difference is notable at the very borderline. Why this should be so I don't really know, but Oregon has a vibration of harmony with Nature; Nevada, one of taking, not giving; Mexico, a warm heart quality. California, by contrast with all three of them, has a vibration of high energy.

As a child I traveled nine times across the Atlantic Ocean, between Romania and America. After the first two days of seasickness, I always exclaimed enthusiastically to my parents, "Oh, Mommy, Daddy, I just *love* the sea!" It had such an expansive effect on my mind.

Always, when traveling, I try to tune in to the vibrations of places. To me, the vibrations are much more interesting than

---

2 Once, the psychic and author James van Praagh entered a redwood forest, of which many of the trees had been felled. He actually heard loud screams all around him. —SK, 2013

the buildings people go to as tourist attractions.

Wherever saints have lived, the spiritual vibrations are very strong. Pilgrimage is beneficial above all for the vibrations that linger in holy spots.[3]

I remember, while I lived at Mt. Washington in Los Angeles where my Guru had located his headquarters, going out to the mountains one day for a bit of skiing. On my way back, I lay with my eyes closed in the back of our pickup truck. All of a sudden I sat up and exclaimed, "It feels all of a sudden so *peaceful!*" We had just driven in through the front gates of Mt. Washington.

To form communities among natural surroundings is certainly more beneficial than to form them in any city.[4] It is also much cheaper, of course, to buy land in the country.

Country living also, by contrast, poses severe disadvantages for the average person. Economic opportunities are relatively few. Most people are not farmers even by inclination. Their skills are city skills: those of the merchant who needs customers

---

3 In Israel for instance, when I went to Capernaum, I tried to dig down mentally through centuried accretions of vibrations. Suddenly I was aware of the still-lingering vibrations of Jesus and his youthful disciples—of their spiritual joy as they sang together of God's love. —SK, 2013

4 An interesting fact is that many of our Ananda communities are located in the hills at a level of about 3,000 feet. One of them is in Mountain View, California (near Palo Alto), in the heart of Silicon Valley, where at least the vibrations are highly intelligent, and open-minded. In fact, in our city centers we have often bought buildings and property in run-down areas, where mostly people of low consciousness had lived, and have built them up. In light of what I have written so far, this may have seemed the worst of all choices. In fact, however, it has worked well for us because low consciousness has little lingering power. Quite soon, in those places, we have lifted their vibrations spiritually and made them beneficial. —SK, 2013

for his wares; of the secretary who can work only if there are letters to type; of the teacher who needs students to teach. Any move on one's own to the country would require total reeducation, and perhaps, for all that, a life of relative uselessness.

And what of social opportunities? If a person has no inclination for farming, he is not likely to want to spend his leisure time hobnobbing with people whose chief interests center on the state of the season's crops.

All these, however, are mere speculations. It was in 1967 that I bought the first land for Ananda. Never has living in the country been a hardship for us. When any need has arisen, we've always found some member who had an aptitude for it, or the necessary experience. I myself am no farmer, no carpenter or builder—no "country boy" in the usual sense of the word at all. I've written books and music, taken art photographs, and am a born leader in the sense that I myself understand leadership: the ability to inspire others to work together with enthusiasm on any needed project; one who sees that job as one of service to others; and one who genuinely *likes* others.

What comes with difficulty on one's own, I have found, is accomplished with relative ease in a group. Persons of like interest, banding together in communities, preserving their independence but working interdependently—each, perhaps with some modifications, contributing his accustomed skills to the whole—under such circumstances, there is no reason why the city person need feel out of place.

Consider, in this context, the simple question of artistic and intellectual opportunities.

In variety, small communities cannot compete with the cities. The greatest satisfaction in the arts, however, lies in creating, not merely in being entertained. In this area of life, the intentional community could offer incomparably more than the big city: the time to create, an interested audience, inspiring natural surroundings, and an opportunity to explore and develop one's inner life.

Nor need a variety of stimulation be lacking. A community accustomed to good libraries would find sufficient incentive to create at least an adequate library of its own. Outside lecturers could be invited to come and speak. An occasional outing to the city to attend a symphony concert or an art exhibit would afford as much cultural exposure as most city dwellers ever get.

There is no earthly reason why a community seeking a natural way of life should utterly reject the benefits of modern civilization. Perfect isolation would be economically unsound, even if it were in some way desirable. Unless one wanted to revert to some sort of Neanderthal existence, complete self-sufficiency would mean that a community would have to produce, at enormous expense, all of its own machinery, its plumbing fixtures, its cooking and eating utensils, its clothing fabrics, even its own toothpaste. Considering how inexpensive such items are in our society, because produced on a mass scale, it seems only practical for a community to devote itself to selling what it can on the outside, and to buying what it needs with the profit.

The community might, in short, be similar in many ways to any village, with the basic distinction that it would be an *intentional* community. It would be based on cooperation, not competition; on self-unfoldment rather than on self-aggrandizement at the expense of one's fellow beings. Competitiveness is a greatly overvalued quality; I would go so far as to call it a spiritual fault.

Basic, however, to the success of any community is the question of income. People living together cooperatively in the country could grow their own food, build their own buildings, perhaps make their own clothes. Many of the materials even for these basic necessities, however, would have to be brought in from outside. They would need an income with which to buy them.

What possible sources of income would there be for a community that lived well outside the busy industrial centers? The problem is less difficult than it may seem.

Presumably, persons coming to live in the community would bring with them certain skills, for some of which—wood carving, painting, weaving, sandal-making, pottery—there would be a ready market in the nearby towns. More likely, they would involve practical trades, such as building and carpentry, and white-collar skills such as typing, merchandising, and teaching. Because few persons are equipped with skills that would assist survival in the remote wilderness, and because most of those with a yen to hie away to distant mountain ranges are probably temperamentally unsuited anyway to living communally, it seems wise to consider buying land not very far from the mainstream of civilization.

Specialization is the hallmark of our age. It should not be difficult for creative minds to find some sort of industry in which the community could specialize, offering its product at a competitive price to the industrial, building, or mercantile world. This industry could even be sophisticated—the manufacture, for example, of electronic devices. Indeed, in the age of burgeoning computers many people could, and do, live out in the country *as individuals.*

Books could be published, clothing made; records produced; a mail-order business developed: all of these could bring income to the community. Teachers could go out even to distant parts of the world with the message of the value to society of communities.

A major source of income could be weekend programs and seminars for outsiders.

Another possible source of income, and something that would in any case be necessary, would be a school for children. A school run on creative and idealistic lines should attract students from outside the community. Indeed, I have written a book on this subject, called *Education for Life.* It has appeared in many languages, and inspired the creation of many schools based on its principles.

The community could also create its own dramas, pageants, and other artistic and spiritual entertainments, which it could offer to clubs, schools, and colleges around the country.

Builders in the community could go beyond the community and build homes for people living elsewhere.

I keep on saying "could." In fact, all these things, and many more, are what Ananda has already done.

There is no reason why the community could not also open its own shops in larger communities nearby. Integrity of workmanship, and lower costs resulting from the elimination of middlemen, should make it possible to win for its products a good enough reputation to ensure their commercial success.

Basic to the economic success of a cooperative community would be the simple principle of cooperation. In the big cities, every man is obliged to compete for his place in the sun. Out of a thousand people, each has, potentially, 999 rivals. Anxiety, tension, frustration—such are a few of the known side effects. But consider also how much time and energy are devoted in ordinary business to outmaneuvering, outbidding, and out-shouting the other fellow, and how much money is spent for the ungenerous purpose of drawing shoppers away from his door to one's own.

Much has been written about the benefits of a competitive system. Certainly, the huge socialistic monopoly that is normally posed as an alternative, while it may result in less material waste, affords also less human incentive. But what of the small intentional community, where *voluntary cooperation* is taught as an alternative to both competition and monopoly?

Supposing that out of a thousand people, each person had, not 999 rivals, but as many potential friends and colleagues.

There is no reason why this should not be possible in a community that emphasized cooperation as a way of life.[5]

Cooperation, however, rightly understood, ought not by any means to be limited to the community. It should reach out to embrace the larger "community" of mankind. Hence, of course, Yogananda's term, "orld brotherhood colony."

In India, the devout Hindu is taught, before eating a meal, to pour a libation of gratitude onto the ground from which the food has come; to give food to an animal, since it is with the help of animals that man obtains food; and to feed some hungry stranger whose position, but for his own good fortune, he might himself be sharing. Side by side, similarly, with a search for personal and communal prosperity, there should develop a sense of responsibility to society at large, without the existence of which the community would very likely be little more than a primitive tribe.

Instead of competition with the outside world, there should develop a sense of sharing with it. One important contribution might be that of example.

Two donkeys were harnessed by a peasant to move a rock. But the animals pulled in opposite directions. Although they

---

5 Does this sound like an "impossible dream"? Ananda Village is now old enough to claim to have withstood the test of time. The harmony within this community of several hundred members, and also with those outside the community with whom we deal, is legendary. So also is the level of prosperity legendary among experimental communities. Assuredly, cooperation is no merely utopian dream.

A number of intentional communities in the past, also, demonstrated considerable financial stability. Where they failed, the fault was due largely to an impractical effort to isolate themselves, or to too idealistic an expectation of human nature. —SK, 1988 worked themselves to exhaustion, the rock was not moved an inch. What of a community where men have learned to act in a spirit of cooperation, not of ceaseless competition—where a little labor suffices to feed many mouths? Would such an example be totally lost on society at large?

Rome and Carthage, fighting one another to their mutual destruction, set an example for the ages of the uselessness of selfish greed. Better than ten negative examples, however, is one positive solution. What of a community that views others not as competitors, nor as strangers, but as friends? Such a community, even if removed from the vortices of civilization, could be a more forceful influence for good than a dozen institutions that were more "involved," but also more submerged, in urban insanities.

Chapter Four
INTENTIONAL COMMUNITIES, PAST AND PRESENT

A remark that one often hears with respect to cooperative communities is, "So many have been started, but all of them have failed." This statement is simply not true. Actually, there have been a number of spectacular successes.

The Inspirationists of Amana, the Harmonists at Economy, the Mennonites, the Shakers, the Hutterites—these names are well known to history. They were wealthy. Some of them are still flourishing. That others eventually died out—often after decades, or even after one or two centuries—need no more be termed a failure than the fact that almost all business concerns eventually die defines them as failures. The way of life is ever to grow, and then die. Without eventual death, room would never be made for new forms of life. Any institution that endures through the ages, indeed, is probably only a shell of its former self. At some point in its history, instead of dying, it must have chosen to become petrified.

In our own age we have only to look at the kibbutzim of modern Israel to see a vital, flourishing movement that, for all its ups and downs, cannot in any way be termed a failure.

And there are the monasteries, similar in many ways, if not

in all, to the intentional communities I propose here. Indeed, what community could be more intentional than a monastery?

It would be wise to consider briefly various communal experiments, and to study the reasons why some of them failed, while others succeeded.

Often, as we have already said, the unsuccessful experiments were founded on too idealistic a view of human nature. A reading of *Kibbutz,* by Melford E. Spiro, conveys the impression that even the modern kibbutzim, while in themselves a decided success, have proved disillusioning to some of their members, who expected their way of life to evolve the "perfect" man. Rousseau's concept of the "noble savage" reads well in print, but one encounters this wonderful creature too rarely here on ignoble earth. The jungle savage is often, in fact, *less* noble than his city counterpart. The belief that a return to nature will automatically produce good people is naïve. The ensuing disappointment can well prove shattering.

Linked to too idealistic a view of human nature was the failure of communities—devastating to any but the best established—to screen their applicants. Robert Owen, in founding a utopian community at New Harmony, Pennsylvania, did not take into account the danger of mixing people of diverse convictions. His community lasted only three years.

Perhaps one of the greatest mistakes that community planners made was to attempt too much with their plans. No system can create virtue. The most it can do is facilitate the development of virtue. For virtue is a development that must always spring from the good will of the individual members. "Freeland," a community founded in the 1890s on the basis of a book by the Austrian economist, Theodor Hertzka, failed largely for this reason. In trying to adhere too closely to Hertzka's elaborate blueprint, the community finally foundered in disillusionment.

A common failing of new communities has been the tendency to demand too radical a change of their members. In biology there is an axiom that nature never proceeds by sudden leaps. This is certainly true, with very rare exceptions, of human nature. Leniency must be granted people, within reason, to grow at their own speed.

Another defect in certain communal experiments has been a tendency to isolationism. A group of people that seek to cut off all ties with the outside world will find themselves forced to work tirelessly simply to produce the bare necessities. The first generation may be inspired, in reaction against modern life, to withdraw to such extremes. But unless their children are kept exceedingly uninformed, the chances are that when they grow up they will want to return to the cities, where at least one does not have to slave like a beast of burden merely to remain alive.

The consensus of persons who have made a study of community life is that some definite communal structure is needed. Coupled to this advice, one always finds mentioned the need for strong leadership. People who are left to drift their own ways soon drift apart. A chicken with its head chopped off will run about erratically. A typical example of the problems encountered by societies that are ruled too rigidly by consensus was the unfortunate Icarian community, whose president was not free even to buy a sack of wheat without the specific consent of the whole community. Even people with the best of intentions require coordination in a group endeavor, but not total uniformity. The best that can come of rigid rule by consensus is an uninspired community in which every inching step forward is applauded as a giant leap.

Communities that have failed have done so, finally, because they lacked a clearly defined sense of purpose. A mere wish for economic stability does not seem to have been enough of a motive to inspire people to remain united. It is no accident that, of the successful ventures, nearly all have been spiritually inspired.

How, then, might the pitfalls we have outlined be avoided?

First, one should not expect miracles. It is enough if a new way of life be *better* than the old one. It is too much to ask that it also be perfect.

Policies pertaining to the acceptance of applicants are important. One carping faultfinder in a community can undermine the morale of many well-intentioned members. It would be wise, especially in a new community, to take care that only harmonious persons be admitted.

Again, there should be some system, some rules, but not with a view to any such rule creating goodness in people. The vital concern should be for people as individuals, and not as parts of a system. Some sort of system will be needed only to coordinate the life of the community, not to be its salvation.

People should not be expected to embrace a way of life that is too radically different from the one to which they are presently accustomed. This caution is important especially from the standpoint of enforcing "togetherness." A community of like minds cannot be forged on the strength of any mere theory. People must grow to a sense of unity naturally. The safest course for a new community, especially, would be to allow each person the freedom to meet others on his own terms.

Finally, for a community to be intentional there must be some sort of leadership. Emerson wrote, "An institution is the lengthened shadow of one man." Such, throughout history, has nearly always been the case. A leader, however, is not a dictator. He encourages initiative on the part of others. He places human values ahead of any system, and inspires people towards their own self-unfoldment.

The less tight-knit a community, the greater the chances of its having this type of a leader. Where people are expected to do everything in common, however, and to be of one mind on every issue, frictions can mount quickly. A community that strives for constant, intense "togetherness" will require miracles of leadership to survive.

Consider, then, another type of community: the normal village, where "togetherness" is not driven down people's throats. There, administration is easily kept to a minimum. Such villages have endured where close-knit communities, lacking a strong leadership, have disintegrated.

The obvious solution, if one does not favor a dictatorship,

is simply not to demand from people a constant togetherness, and hence a measure of unanimity, for which they are unprepared. The leadership of a community might then be strong, but not fussy. People would be given the freedom to grow, but at the same time would be given enough of a sense of common direction to help them to grow together, and not apart.

A safe beginning, surely, would be to heed well the fact that nearly all successful colonies have been spiritually oriented. If the idea of "world brotherhood colonies" is to spread, it would be well for at least the initial experiments not to be planned without including this (so far) all-but-essential ingredient.

A religious orientation, however, need not imply sectarianism. The essence of religion is its emphasis on an *inner* life. It is not because of religious fanaticism that communities have held together, but because the inner life developed in their members, through their faith, has given them the peace of mind to smile away petty annoyances, the flexibility to meet others partway on disagreements, and the freedom to enjoy things without attachment. In the matter of emphasizing an inner life, no community can afford to be lax, even if its goals are not otherwise spiritual. It is to make an inner life possible that cooperative communities are needed in the first place.

Chapter Five
HOW TO BEGIN

I read once in a newspaper about someone who had been trying to start an ideal community, complete with progressive university, laboratories, concert halls—all the social amenities, in short, styled in impeccable architectural taste. He was trying to raise two and a half billion dollars for this dream-venture. Needless to say, the dream never materialized. Two and one-half billion dollars is hardly a pittance! Anyone with such an impractical scheme would be lucky to raise two and a half thousand. No one wants to sail his money on the North Wind.

This example is worthy of notice, however. For people too often imagine that huge sums will be necessary for a worthy project to be launched, and before people can be brought together to work on it. This is true, no doubt, for some ventures—Disneyland, for example, which couldn't have been started without a huge initial investment. For intentional communities, however, the very opposite is true. People, by working together, produce wealth. Many great ventures, indeed, have started on a shoestring. Nor did Walt Disney himself start out in the world with the money to finance his future success.

Often, it is better to make a beginning with little than to

spend years waiting for the skies to rain gold.

Others I have heard of, wealthy men, bought land with the intention of developing it for the future enjoyment of many people. Theirs were charitable ventures, from which others were expected to benefit with a minimum of responsibility on the part of the members.

These men were at least in a position to build. But the willingness of people to accept their patronage, without assuming personal responsibility for the success or failure of the project, would spell sure death to any community. Even if people did work under such a scheme, what would their motive be? Gratitude? There is a point beyond which gratitude can become another word for slavery.

No, it is better for people to own their own venture, and to work for it secure in the knowledge that by so doing they are working for themselves.

One way to get started would be for interested persons to save toward the initial costs. It is not all that difficult nowadays for people to save up for things they really want. A hundred people each saving $1,000 would have $100,000—enough to make a very good beginning.

There are ways to make it easier to convert good intentions into reality. Consider this suggestion: Institute a "crash program" for several months. People can save considerably more than usual if they adopt the cooperative principle from the start, pooling their resources. Young people, especially, would find it easy to adapt themselves to such a scheme.

They could share their meals in common. The diet, during this period, might be simplified. Cooking for many would greatly reduce costs and labor. A set fee could be paid by each participant for expenses. Cooking could either be done by rotation on a voluntary basis, or paid for, the cooks raising their own $1,000 through their work in the kitchen. Whatever money is left over from the expense account could be used to buy grain for later use by the community.

Housing accommodations could be shared temporarily. To share one's room or apartment with others may not appeal to some people, but for a limited period of time it needn't prove a great hardship for people whose ideal is to live in community.

If this plan were not adopted, a regular weekly or monthly payment towards membership in the cooperative might ensure a more rapid saving than hoarding the money oneself against the day when this sum reaches the predetermined figure. ($300 in the bank, and a Sears Roebuck catalog by one's bed, can perform magic vanishing acts!)

The above suggestions, while reasonable enough in theory, demand a degree of faith, a firmness of purpose, and a clarity of vision that one rarely, if ever, encounters in large groups of people. Many people will get behind a venture once it has proved successful. Few, however, are visionary enough to dedicate themselves with indomitable energy to a dream, especially to one for which there are not as yet many successful models. Ironically, while it takes manpower to make a communitarian dream successful, few people will join a communitarian venture until they see it already well on the road to success.

The more developed a venture of this type becomes, however, the greater the numbers of people who will get behind it. It seems wisest, therefore, to get the project "off the ground" as soon as possible, even with one broken wing, than to wait, discuss endlessly, and plan toward the Perfect Day.

If it is difficult to get large groups of people behind a reasonable plan for success, it is, unfortunately, even more difficult to persuade groups to back a "broken wing" type of beginning. Thus, it may prove necessary for a new community to be launched by a bare handful of individuals, inspired, perhaps, by only one person with the dream and the determination to get the project "off the ground" despite every caution by the worldly wise that the thing simply can't be done.

In this case, the secret will lie in involving people stage by stage. Where they might be frightened off by the sheer magnitude of the project, were it presented to them as the creation of a thriving intentional village, it may prove relatively easy to invite their cooperation in constructing a less ambitious project—a place, say, for retreat, or for summer camping. The village itself could develop stage by stage, from a summer camp or a place of occasional retreat to a place with a small permanent staff, and so on, each step being taken as people feel ready for it.

In founding Ananda Village, I had to earn most of the initial money, and much of it for several subsequent years, myself. One really has no call to complain if, in trying to do something for others, he finds their help somewhat elusive until the project is already off to a good start.

At first, many people evidently thought I wanted to take advantage of them. I remember my first venture at earning money for the project. I put out a record album of songs, hoping it would help finance the first step I envisioned toward the community: the building of a meditation retreat.

"So you can make lots of money, eh?" leered a popular talk show host on whose program I appeared, hoping to promote the album.

The first meeting I called of possibly interested people to discuss the project dissolved in accusations of suspected bad faith on my part.

The only way to proceed proved to be to take all the initial risks myself, while gradually involving more and more people in different aspects of the project as we went along, so they would not feel it was my project, but theirs. This, I feel, was important. It would never have done for me to do all the work for them. Group involvement is necessary in any group undertaking.

I remember an experience I had as a child. I'd been given a bicycle for my birthday. I was so happy to get this present that I spent most of my birthday party teaching the other children to ride. What I did was hold the bicycle by the seat and the handlebar, as the other child pedaled cautiously. When I felt that he had his balance and had developed a sense of confidence, I released the handlebar but kept my grip on the seat. My next step was to release the seat, but keep running beside the bicycle until its rider saw that he could go on without me. After that, he took off, gaily shouting over his shoulder, "Look at me!"

If more than one person assumes the task of founding a community, their approach must be similar: not to hold the reins too firmly, but as much as possible to involve those who come later onto the scene. The community must be seen to be theirs, as much as that of the founders.

Let us assume that the necessary initial sum has been raised. How, then, to proceed?

A good rule, based on the experience of other communities in the past, is: Don't borrow beyond a reasonable expectation of your ability to repay. Remember that the community's income will be uncertain to begin with.

At Ananda Village we were forced to borrow, but I never took a loan without personally assuming the burden of repayment—at least up to the time when I felt it was realistic to expect others to assume some, and then gradually more, of the load. It meant hard work for me, but nothing worthwhile was ever accomplished by laziness.

It would be wise, as I mentioned earlier, not to buy land too far away from settled areas. The community will need income, and will depend on its contacts with society at large to obtain it. It might even be wise not to settle too far away from the members' original home.

San Francisco residents, for example, would find land cheaper in Oregon than in their own area, but—assuming that they need to begin the development on a part-time basis—it would also be more difficult for them to visit Oregon regularly. Worse still, the greater distance would greatly reduce the chances of drawing new recruits from their present circle of acquaintances.

Most people would want to see the place before agreeing to live in it. Willing workers will be the community's greatest source of wealth. Why jeopardize that source by an initial saving, at the cost of continued accessibility?

If possible, land should be bought in sufficient quantity to permit future expansion, or in an area which holds a promise of future land acquisition.

Although a new cooperative community will not face the hardships of a single couple starting out on their own in the woods, the standard of living will certainly not compare with that which most of the members have known in the city. The first stages of community life will have to be for people in whom the pioneering spirit is strong. Newcomers should be prepared in advance for a life of unaccustomed simplicity.

The labor of years will bring wealth. But need an exaggerated simplicity to begin with be a burden? Surely not! For anyone who knows to its heart the bustle and complexity of big-city living, a simple life can mean only welcome release from burdensome nonessentials for things more basic to one's happiness.

As much as possible of the community's initial capital should be kept free for investment in various profitable ventures. The first residents may be content for some time to live in tents.

A practical, and more comfortable, alternative would be the Navajo Indian *hogan*: Secondhand beams can be bought inexpensively, arranged in a large circular pattern, narrowed slowly to form a rounded roof with an opening in the center, then covered with plastic and chicken wire, then with adobe. A moveable plastic dome can be put over the opening at the top. For very little money one can have a remarkably roomy, comfortable, and well-insulated home!

Crops should be planted as early as possible. If the community is not so fortunate as to have a farming expert among its members, those in charge of the farming should have the soil tested to ascertain its quality, and get advice on how to improve it, if necessary. It would be wise to plan the crops for at least two years in advance.

One advantage of eating one's own produce will be readily appreciated by anyone who has had a chance to dine on a farm. Really fresh fruits and vegetables are a delight simply unknown to those who are forced to eat their food hours, even days, after it has been picked.

As insurance against future crop failures, the community should plan from the start to gather and store supplies of whole grain, split peas, lentils, and other nonperishable foods.

One of the most expensive, and least healthful, items in the average food budget is meat. A community will be fortunate if it can agree to be vegetarian, at least as far as its own production and official consumption are concerned (leaving room, that is, for the individual who craves meat enough to buy it for himself on the outside). Reasons for a meatless diet are given in my book, *Yoga Postures for Higher Awareness*.

A community may be surprised to discover how little money it actually requires for food. In 1950, I ate for some months on $7.50 a month, buying all my food at the grocery store. In 1960 I mentioned this feat to some friends. (They had been exclaiming on the high price of food.)

"Oh, but in 1950 everything was different!" they assured me.

Perhaps so. But in 1963 I kept a similar budget for three months. Actually, it came to $10 a month, but roughly $2.50 of this amount went for desserts and other nonessentials. All I did was omit from my diet the more expensive items: meat (which I have not eaten since I was in my early twenties), eggs, bread, butter, milk. Instead of bread, I ground my own flour and made an unleavened flat bread, like a tortilla. Frying this "chapatti" (as it is called in India) in oil, I needed no butter. I trained my palate to like powered milk, which costs only a third as much as regular milk. I sprouted alfalfa seeds, ate nuts, fruits, and vegetables, made an occasional thick curried soup, or *daal,* of split peas or lentils. Raw fruits and vegetables gave me a maximum of nourishment in a minimum of bulk.

Inflation has raised the cost of everything since then. Still, one may be astonished at how well he can live on relatively little, if he is forced to, or sufficiently motivated to try.

"The fruit of luxury," wrote Thoreau, "is luxury." The fruits of simple living, on the other hand, are peace, happiness, and freedom. For many people, it would be no deprivation at all to live without modern conveniences, perhaps with gaslights, and with wood or oil stoves, and no telephone or television!

There is a story of an American Indian who supported his family by tilling a little plot of soil less than an acre in size. He was befriended by a neighbor, a wealthy white farmer. This man, pitying his poor friend for his meager subsistence, offered him several acres of adjoining land as a gift.

"You are kind," answered the Indian. "But see: The land I have is quite enough for our needs. If I had more to till, when would I find time for singing?"

If men would only simplify their needs, how much time might they not find to sing!

Chapter Six
COMMUNAL ECONOMICS

A vital question facing the cooperative society is that of the apportionment of wealth. The classical plan, dating as far back as apostolic days, has been for the members to own all things in common. Under this system, the individual has the use of whatever he receives from the community, but he may not consider it his personal property. In monasteries, the practice has been to refer even to personal items such as sandals as "our sandals." In return for his work, the member receives everything free of charge.

In a monastic community this system has been found to work. Freedom from attachment to money and property is desirable, moreover, in one whose life is devoted to the spiritual search. But where families are concerned, I think this system is unnecessarily restrictive, and out of keeping with the consciousness of our age. It is also a real obstacle to the development of the community's economy. Even in monasteries, this practice discourages initiative, and encourages a passive dependency—questionable benefits, even in a religious calling.

The great problem with total communal ownership is that it increases the need for communal discipline. People who re-

ceive everything without paying for it must be induced somehow to work for what they get. Without the motive of personal
profit, the only solution, if the community is to be productive
at all, is to stress either group "spirit," or the beauty of holy
obedience. Advantage is too often taken of the resident's good
will. He comes for a life of peace, and in the name of group
spirit finds himself launched on all sorts of glorious projects:
the construction of a new library, a hospital, a recreation center—and not just any kind of buildings, but, for the sake of the
community's good name, the best imaginable.

A community I know in India, seized with this noble motive, has devoted decades to constructing a temple that—such
is the dream—will be more beautiful than the Taj Mahal. To
what purpose?

If people were all highly spiritual, there would be no need
to regiment them to make sure that they work. Nor would
there be any danger lest zealous leaders regiment them so much
that they *over*work. In fact, according to certain scriptures, if
all people were truly spiritual they would be sustained without
having to work at all. Whether or not that will ever be the case,
it is clear that we are not living at present in such a spiritual age.

It is not surprising that, in Russia, where only 3 percent of
the cultivated land is privately owned, this tiny portion supplies
fully half of all the nation's meat, milk, and green vegetables.

The early American colonies had a similar experience. Most
people need to feel that they are working for themselves. They
may actually be doing so just as much in a totally communistic

society, but their vision is seldom broad enough clearly to grasp the fact.

Nor, it must be added, is the vision of communism's leaders any clearer. These persons tend, in most cases, to accept the worker's contribution as a matter of course, while remaining painfully conscious of the fact that, in addition to the burden of supervising his work, they must also feed, clothe, house, and entertain him. Small wonder that the benefits with which they supply him tend to be minimal and drab. And small wonder that he is treated to harsh discipline, and told that he must obey always, and never think of himself or of his personal needs.

And if, in the case of a small communistic society, a member ever should leave, what will his recompense be? He will very likely be told that his stay there was permitted as a favor to him, that the community owes him nothing—save, perhaps, a reprimand for his ingratitude. After that, he may be given a pittance, out of "charity."

Thus it is—final indignity!—that many a monk or nun, and many a member of a completely communal society, has stayed on in the community not out of high ideals, but simply out of economic need. In this way, he passes his latter days in frustration, infecting others with his fits of irrational temper and his jealous pride of seniority. It is a situation comparable to that in *No Exit*, that thoroughly depressing play by Jean-Paul Sartre, the hopeless moral of which is, "Hell is other people."

No, the soundest course, it seems to me, would be to follow the pattern to which people are in any case accustomed:

Let them work for wages, and in turn pay for whatever they receive. Let them save what they like for the future. "The best government," Thoreau claimed, "is that which governs least." The simplest management in a community is as much as possible to give people the incentive to manage themselves. At Ananda Village we've always tried to keep the decision-making process at a grassroots level. When people must look out for their own needs, they will bestir themselves well enough to produce.

There is another advantage in this method: In the usual communistic society, and in the usual homogeneous community, the tendency is, as we have seen, to force people to overwork. If, however, a man must pay for everything he gets, it will be for him to decide how much income he really needs, and how many hours a week, in consequence, he must work. Under this system, if he wants to devote hours every day to painting or to meditating, he will have greater freedom to do so.

The difference between the economic system here proposed and a normal system of free enterprise is that here the member remains, as in any cooperative, a part owner of the community. Whether in higher wages, discounts, stock dividends, or special benefits, he receives his share of the community's prosperity. It is up to him, by the contribution of his labor, to increase that prosperity or to keep it lower.

Much is made in capitalistic societies of the advantages of capitalism over communism. In fact, it seems to me, mankind is still struggling toward the ideal solution. Capitalism is certainly preferable to communism. The difference, however, is one of degree, not one of polar opposites.

Capitalism is a form of absentee landlordism. Think back to the period in France before the French Revolution. The aristocracy wanted to live luxuriously at court. They saw their properties, and the peasants working those properties, purely in the light of support for their wasteful living. The welfare of the peasants meant nothing to most of them. They rarely, if ever, saw the people from whose labor they derived their income.

Is there not a certain parallel, here, to the modern capitalistic system? Without capital no company can flourish, and this capital typically must be raised by selling shares in the company. The company's employees are not serfs in the same sense as the French peasants were. Nevertheless, those who buy stock in a company have little interest, typically, in the welfare of the workers. All they want is profits.

Wouldn't a more ideal system be one in which the workers themselves owned the company? Their interest in it would be more all-round. They would see it not only in terms of profit, but in terms of creating a pleasant working environment, products in which they could take pride, the satisfaction of being individually responsible for the growth of the company.

Such would be the benefit of living under the economic system of an intentional community.

Specifically, the system recommended here might be described as follows:

Work done for the community would be paid for, if possible, according to the member's recognized needs. Some of the community income would be earned through community-owned enterprises. The rest of it should come from a tax levied on community members and on privately owned businesses.

Private enterprise should be allowed. Enterprising members should be encouraged to form their own industries or businesses, always with the community's consent, and to employ others at wages that they can afford to pay. All members should be encouraged to contribute as much as possible voluntarily to the well-being of all.

To prevent anyone with sufficient wealth from controlling the community, the normal practice of cooperatives should be followed: Each member should have only one vote, regardless of how much money he puts into the community. For full voting membership, however, a person must make a minimum investment. At Ananda Village, the present membership fee is $1,500 for single persons, and $2,500 for couples.

Every resident should be expected to pay monthly toward utilities, maintenance, and improvements, as well as toward taxes and any mortgage on the land.

Chapter Seven
COMMUNALISM VS. PRIVACY

Most spokesmen for the idea of cooperative communities have made it a point to emphasize the efficiency involved in feeding and housing everyone communally. B. F. Skinner, in *Walden Two*, wrote that if it were not for such communal facilities, the community he described would be "occupying some two hundred and fifty dwelling houses and working in a hundred offices, shops, stores, and warehouses. It's an enormous simplification and a great saving of time and money."

But life offers many other satisfactions besides those that may be gleefully relished in saving time and money. I myself, when leaving the apartment I had in San Francisco on an errand, would often go out of my way to drive through Golden Gate Park. It may have been a waste in terms of time and gasoline, but the gain to my spirits made the detour worthwhile to me.

No, to say that people *must* live together for any theoretical reason would be a mistake, as indeed it would also be to say they *must* live alone. For many an individual, a house and a garden of his own epitomizes the "good life."

Granted, a completely communal life *would* be economical. Shared facilities should certainly be provided for those people who prefer them, and perhaps recommended to all. Anyone who would rather live in his own home, however, should be allowed the freedom to do so. If he wishes to eat there, too, that should be his concern. But if, on the other hand, he prefers the ease and economy of eating with others, there is no reason why there should not be a communal dining room where he can join them.

A cohesive spirit should develop in a natural way, and not because of some theory wielded over the heads of the residents like a sledgehammer.

While members of the community should be granted a right to have homes of their own, however, newcomers might well be required to live communally for the first year. Objectionable characteristics would be more quickly observable. For the welfare of the community, only persons of reasonably harmonious disposition should be admitted to full residency.

A limit should be placed on the amount of land an individual is allowed for his private use. A person or a family who live apart should be allowed only as much as they require for their building, with a small garden besides to protect their privacy.

In the early years at Ananda Village new members, fresh from city life, wanted to build as far from one another as possible. An abundance of land permitted a fairly wide dispersion of dwellings. In time, however, they came to the realization that they'd been isolating themselves, not from faceless strangers, but from friends, whose proximity they enjoyed.

In 1976, a devastating forest fire destroyed twenty out of

twenty-one homes. In many ways, unnecessary to enumerate here, the devastation proved a blessing. From a standpoint of village planning, it enabled us to rebuild as we would have built in the first place, had we had sufficiently clear foresight.

Ananda as it was reconstructed followed a new plan of cluster housing, with the homes standing 100–150 feet from one another. Large areas of land are now open for the enjoyment of all, rather than being vaguely defined as "so-and-so's" territory simply because his home was somewhere in the vicinity.

The land should belong to the community as a whole, not to individuals. At Ananda it was found necessary, in order to avoid being classified as a condominium (the law regarding condominiums is quite strict), to keep title to the homes also in the name of the community.

Houses might all be constructed according to an accepted type. The heterogeneous impression given by so many American cities is due largely to their profusion of their architectural styles. Community planning, moreover, should be directed with a view to future growth—an obvious point except for one observation: I believe that the problem, in time, will be one of too many people rather than too few.

If the signs have been read correctly, we have entered a period in history when thousands will be drawn to this communal way of life. Paramhansa Yogananda wrote in terms of hundreds, even thousands, joining a single community. An *intentional* community of thousands, while almost certainly unacceptable to most people interested in communities today, would still be immensely preferable to the confusion of cross-currents that exists in the large cities.

A *Self-realization* community would probably elect to divide, however, long before it reached a population that was too unwieldy. One or two, or possibly a few, hundred residents might prove to be the preferred maximum. An eventual division should indeed be anticipated, and even desired, from the start. For it would be better to have many small communities in different parts of the country, where local people can visit them and benefit by observation from this new way of life, than one large community in a single place, knowable to most people only through hearsay. Better in any case a small community. Excessive size will deprive it of much of its original charm.

Let us consider, then, the case of an eventual division. For years I maintained that the ideal would be for branch communities to be autonomous. In this way, I believed, it would be possible to avoid the cumbersome system of centricity, wherein the head office sets the directions for its branches, and may feel it necessary to impose policies that are locally unsuitable.

In earlier editions of this book, I suggested "the 'colonists,' as we might call them, might be given their share out of the funds of the parent community, and perhaps also a loan without interest, and sent off on their own to found, not a branch, but another autonomous body. For no community of this nature can be guided practically from a distance. A new community might be under the 'wing' of the parent for a time, but it must strive at the earliest possible opportunity to become independent."

As the time came for Ananda Village to start branch centers, however, it quickly became obvious that my projections were unrealistic. For one thing, the kind of members who might have been happy to go off on their own were in no case those whom we would have chosen to send, as representatives of our way of life and of our philosophy. In fact, small groups of members have elected, from time to time, to go off on their own and found communities that they envisioned as more in tune with their ideals. They have gone off with the community's blessings and good will. So far, however, none of these ventures has ever been successful.

Those members, on the other hand, whom we considered competent to start branch centers wanted, in distancing themselves from Ananda, to affirm even more deeply their connection with the community as a whole. They didn't want autonomy.

A further objection to my original plan of division therefore never arose. Nevertheless it can be pointed out: How would a member's financial share in the community ever be computed? It is not like owning so many shares in a corporation. In this sense, it is not even like the worker-owned corporation I proposed earlier. Frankly, the magnitude of the problem, were it ever to arise, would very likely prove mindboggling. At Ananda, the question has been sidestepped by placing all communal property under the ownership of a nonprofit corporation.

The problem of insensitive imposition of guidance from

headquarters, one that is often encountered in corporations with many subsidiary branches, has not arisen to date at Ananda. Here, the personal ties felt by the community with its representatives—even with those in branches as far away from California as Italy—have made collaboration exceptionally harmonious and mutually nourishing.

Even if the future should present difficulties in this regard, it seems likely at this point that a unified organization will prove preferable to a system of autonomy for each group.

Whatever the future holds, the motive spirit behind each community as a whole should be the same as that which would attract the individual to it: *Self-realization.*

And the spirit prevailing among the different colonies should be the same as that which prevails among their individual members: *cooperation.*

Chapter Eight
EDUCATION

"As the twig inclineth, so doth the tree grow."

Education plays a vital role in any community. A cooperative community represents not only new opportunities for better living, but also a new outlook on life, one that can be developed most easily during childhood. But if the children are sent off to neighboring schools, the competitive spirit that is encouraged there will not advance their understanding of co-operation. Children are more inclined to imitate than to think things out for themselves.

The community should strive, then, as early as possible to build schools of its own—institutions where children can be taught how to *live,* not only how to add and subtract and recite from a catalogue of dry facts.

I have many friends in the teaching profession. It is surprising how many of them grumble at the public school system. Their chief complaint is that they have so little opportunity to be creative. The greater the size of any institution, the greater the need, often, for imposing uniformity on its members. Eccentricity is anathema to any established order.

In a small cooperative school, however, there would be opportunity for endless creativity. Teaching could be a constant experiment with new and better ways of imparting knowledge and understanding.

With an attractive approach to education, there is no reason why group training, of a sort, should not begin early in life, with specially trained "babysitters." Modern social conditioning may influence people to feel that a mother ought to be with her children all the time. But why? When she is busy with her housework she is not in any case free to play with them. They are merely in the way. The time that she can actually devote to them, after her housework has been finished, may be marred by the memory of a long day of scoldings and spankings.

My own early years were spent in Rumania, where my father worked as an oil geologist. Living there, my parents, as Americans, were able to afford a nurse. I often heard them remark that the freedom her assistance gave them made it possible for them to enjoy us much more than they would have done otherwise. And, looking at the matter from our standpoint as children, I can truthfully say that it would be difficult to imagine a happier childhood, or a greater feeling of love and respect than we felt for our parents.

Communal schooling from an early age will also help to accomplish something for which every wise parent should strive: expanding the child's sense of identity. The "us four and no more" attitude is not only selfish, but self-limiting. One of the best reasons for creating intentional communities is that they can help people to expand their sympathies.

To consider again my own childhood, ours also was a quasi-communal life—a number of families fenced in next to a large oil refinery, named, "Teleajen." We each gave special affection to our own parents, but we addressed all the other adults affectionately as "Uncle" and "Auntie."

Why not? The community should be the child's expanded family. Thus, one may well come in time to know all men as his brothers.

It is doubtful whether competitive games and sports can be banned without washing much of the color out of a child's life. But the emphasis, certainly, should be on games in which the child can concentrate on improving his own skills rather than on beating down an opponent.

Grading, similarly, should be done as much as possible on a basis of the teacher's estimate of the child's potential rather than on a scale of comparison with other students. Comparison of one's own mental development with that of anyone else is seldom constructive. (The teacher might, however, assign an objective grade that would be kept in the student's file for future college entrance requirements, and the like.)

Every child should be encouraged to develop according to his own natural bent. Each should select, as a hobby, some special interest or trade. In this field he would receive personal training. (Each member of the community, in fact, would do well to develop some skill that could be offered for the benefit of the community.)

One of the curses of the average school system is the limit it places on creativity. It is no accident that many a creative genius has left his formal education unfinished. For the best way to receive good grades in school is to anticipate the teacher's interests. Girls generally do better than boys simply because they are more skilled in the art of diplomacy. But the trend ought to be just the reverse: It is the teacher who should do his best to find and develop the student's interests.

The chief obstacle to his doing so, usually, is that he has a textbook to follow. As much as possible, in the community's school, teaching should be done from life itself, not from the fixed and brittle dogmas of books.

Each student should be taught also the basic arts of living: how to concentrate; the beauty of kindness and cooperation; how to overcome fear, anger, and jealousy; how to meditate and develop an inner life; how to appreciate the higher values in life. These are not matters for mere theorizing. They will require living situations and wise, personal guidance from the teachers. But they should be a vital part of any "how-to-live" school.

While teaching academic subjects, advantage should be taken of the natural tendency of children toward hero worship. They could be introduced to the lives of great men and women of history, not incidentally only, but as vitally connected with their discoveries and achievements. "A nation is known," Dr. Radhakrishnan, India's Vice President, once remarked to me, "by the men and women it looks upon as great." By the same token, an emphasis on the example of certain great persons can help a child to develop clear ideals. Most children think more easily in terms of persons than of principles.

To suspend a great figure in midair, however, over the barren plains of a vanished era, would not be sufficiently instructive. That person's culture, the general interests of the people of his time, a consideration of the similarities between that age and our own—all these would help in the presentation of academic facts and principles.

In this connection, a pet educational theory of my own has long been to steep the student completely in one subject at a time, instead of obliging him to jump back and forth between completely unrelated fields: French, geometry, American history, and physics.

I remember years ago taking up a study of the fine points of English grammar. For two weeks I did nothing else. In school, a year of scattered classes and homework assignments would have been needed to cover the same ground, and I would have forgotten most of what I had learned within a month after the final exam. Concentration it is that deepens the memory impressions in the brain. The information I absorbed in two weeks of *concentrated* study has remained with me to this day.

If a student could study one subject at a time for periods of, let us say, one month, and vary his mental fare by excursions into *related* fields, I venture to say that he would learn far more, and become far more interested in the process.

A study of algebra, for example, could involve him also in a study of the Arabs, who brought this ancient science from

India. It could touch on the uses of symbolic thinking in real-life situations. It could cover the adventure of modern science, and the great scientists who brought the scientific revolution to pass.

And what matter if, in the course of a year, the same subjects be touched on more than once? Approached several times in relation to different fields of interest, and therefore from different points of view, they should yield new information and wisdom every time.

I do not say that any of the above points is necessary for the development of education in a cooperative community. All of them illustrate, however, an essential feature of any such education: that it be kept free for experimentation.

Chapter Nine
GOVERNMENT

Many utopian writers have given themselves up to dreams of a society without a government. What they have envisioned is a nation in a state of perfect equilibrium, where each person knows his own place. The old Greek, Heraclitus, had an answer for this type of thinking. "All," he said, "is flux." Living organisms achieve perfect equilibrium only in death. Otherwise, all things are in a state of movement. Death itself is only life's way of stepping aside to make way for new life forms.

No, some form of government will always be necessary, and the successes and failures of countless communities suggest that it had better be a strong government. But leadership can be strong without being dictatorial. A dictatorship would be a contradiction from the spirit of a *cooperative* community. Granting the need for a government with the power to act as and when necessary, the best government will still be that which, as Thoreau put it, rules the least. The ideal government is one that encourages personal initiative and responsibility, and that legislates in matters of communal *convenience* rather than of personal outlook and growth.

The fact that man has experimented with so many different types of government suggests that the perfect system yet remains to be found. In fact, as I have already pointed out, no system can be any better than the people whose lives it directs. There can be no "perfect" system, for its members will always be the determining factor in its performance. A system can *facilitate* the expression of goodness in people; it cannot *create* goodness.

Let us, then, look for an efficient government, not a perfect one.

It would be wise for a community to seek not only efficiency, but simplicity in the management of its affairs. And the simplest form of management is supervisory, rather than authoritarian. Members, in other words, should be encouraged as much as possible to make their own decisions, always within a framework of established policy and under the general supervision of the established governing body. Members of this body might be elected annually by resident members.

My experience of life suggests that members should be eligible to vote for membership in the governing body only after they have lived in the community for at least one year. The government would be answerable to the general membership, in which the overall governing power would actually reside.

The officers would consist of a General Manager (whose position would correspond to that of the president of a corporation), a Secretary, and a Treasurer.

In addition, I recommend that there be a Spiritual Director, whose position might correspond roughly to that of Chairman of the Board.

The Spiritual Director would stand back somewhat from the day-to-day affairs of the community, in order constantly to gauge whether government and community intentions were in keeping with the community's basic philosophy. He would actively guide the community and its members toward the fulfillment of their highest ideals.

My reason for recommending a Spiritual Director is that when people are too close to a project, they often lose sight of their ideals. Or else they find themselves compromising an ideal without clearly estimating the cost involved to their first principles. Idealism, not expediency, should be the final arbiter in all community affairs. Hence the importance of not involving the Spiritual Director too directly in practical, day-to-day management. This officer's primary concern should be the community's spiritual welfare. His duty should be to coordinate the community's secular with its spiritual activities, and, by his noninvolvement in secular matters, to preserve an overall view which might otherwise be lost in the exigencies of the moment.

The actual management of ongoing matters, then, would be the duty of the General Manager. He, too, should seek always to keep spiritual principles as the supreme arbiter of his activities. He should therefore be in close communication with the Spiritual Director as regards the general directions taken by the governing body.

It would be counterproductive to spell out too exactly the

relative powers and functions of the different officers, and particularly those of the General Manager and the Spiritual Director. The characters of the individuals in those roles will in any case be the actual determining factor in these matters.

It might be well, however, for neither the office of General Manager nor that of Spiritual Director to be a position open to a general vote by the community. The position of Spiritual Director, especially, ought, I think, to be by appointment on the part of a spiritual directorate consisting of ministers and other members with years of experience in living by the ideals of the community.

The General Manager might be appointed by the elected governing body, in consultation with the Spiritual Director. This position, like that of Spiritual Director, is too important to the far-reaching aims of the community to be filled by a vote of the majority, many of whom, from inexperience, might not have a clear idea of the qualities required for good management. It is important, for example, that mere popularity not be a determining factor in arriving at such decisions.

On the other hand, the community's consent in all decisions is also important. In most cases, particularly when harmony prevails, that consent may be assumed. Should any group of sufficient size—say, five members—request a general referendum on any issue, however, the community should be called together and the issue put to a general vote.

It would be wise, in addition, for the community at large to be consulted on any major decisions—any proposed change of direction for the community; any decision affecting everyone for which no precedent has yet been established; any important new commitment (such as the purpose of property).

The proper balance between experience and the right of all members to be heard and properly represented can be maintained only with sensitivity and in a spirit of sincere friendship for all. Here again, no system could ever guarantee perfection. Ultimately, the smooth working of a community will depend on the spirit of its members, not on its system of government or on its bylaws.

The governing body may appoint individual members of the community to be responsible, as the need arises, for specific areas of community activity. Such positions might include the following, by way of illustration and example:

a. Director of Housing, Parks, and Community Layout

b. Director of Farming and Industrial Planning

c. Director of Entertainment, Recreation, and Cultural Expression

d. Director of Public Relations and Instruction

e. Director of Education and Admissions

f. Director of Public Works

In order that members be selected for these posts primarily on the basis of their spiritual dedication and general executive ability, rather than on a basis of specialized knowledge in any of the above fields, members should be appointed rather than elected to these positions. Subcommittees of specialists might be formed subsequently, under the general coordination of one or another of these Board members.

In all cooperative communities, elections should be held without campaigning, and by secret ballot. Only voting members who are established residents of the community should be allowed to vote in elections of the governing body and on other "in-community" matters. Members who are not established residents might, however, be invited to offer their opinions and suggestions in many matters.

Within the framework outlined above, every member should have the same voting power as any other.

It may be necessary for new communities to grow slowly even into such a simple governmental structure as I have outlined here. For if they plunge too hastily into a cloud of formalities, they may lose sight of the real reason for which they were first drawn together.

Chapter Ten
RULES

Rules should be kept at a minimum. It is far better to establish general customs than hard-and-fast laws. "Too many rules," Yogananda said, "destroy an institution's spirit." Even if everyone follows a rule, the fact that it is a rule makes it fertile soil for gossip and suspicion. ("Did you hear that John *borrowed the garden hose* yesterday?" "Dear God, no!") It acts as a narrowing influence upon the mind, where simple customs might only help everyone to grow harmoniously. It is better, then, to deal as much as possible with individual cases as they arise, and as circumstances dictate, without going on to establish a rule rigidly binding upon a majority who would never consider offending against it anyway.

Certain rules there will have to be, of course. It would be unfair to the newcomer to give him no clear sense of the direction in which the community is proceeding. It would also be difficult for the community to proceed smoothly toward its goals without some definite sense of what those goals were, and how best to reach them. In this respect, certainly, an *intentional* community must differ from the directionless hodgepodge that constitutes the average town or village.

The orientation of an intentional community should be toward the Self-realization of each of its members, and toward a spirit of cooperation. Self-realization is essentially an inward goal. Cooperation implies a spirit that is voluntary, rather than coerced. Both ideals—personal development and group cooperation—imply a respect for one another's rights which leaves no room for egoistic individualism (the kind which carelessly imposes on the freedom of others).

Remember, too, that in an intentional community individual development and group cooperation are interactive principles. The member who sincerely seeks inner development will thereby help the others to become uplifted as well. The member, on the other hand, who makes no effort to improve himself cannot validly claim that his indolence is no one's business but his own. His laziness is a detriment to the sincere efforts of others.

Proscriptive rules should be few. One such rule should definitely take into account the fact that every community so far that has permitted the use of drugs has soon drifted into a sense of communal irresponsibility, the sure precursor of communal disintegration.

It would be wise also to prohibit alcoholic beverages as a useless indulgence among people who are trying to live a better, healthier life.

Smoking might be discouraged without any actual rule being made against it. The members might simply be asked to abstain from smoking in public places, or wherever their smoking might affect others. In all probability the very concept of an intentional community will minimize this problem, if it doesn't eliminate it altogether. The best solution, then, may be not to treat it as a problem.

At Ananda, where most of the members are vegetarian, the question of meat-eating also is treated in this way.

Here are a few suggestions, only, for basic rules that a community might do well to adopt.

1. No job shall be played up as more dignified or important than any other.

2. No one may act in such a way as to harm another. (This rule might be interpreted subtly, as well as literally, for a negative personal example can, in certain cases, be as injurious to a community as actual physical violence.)

3. Voting must be considered a right, but also a privilege, not a duty. No one should vote unless he has formed a definite opinion on the subject under consideration.

4. No hallucinogenic drugs or alcoholic beverages may be taken by any member of the community, whether on or off the community property.

Chapter Eleven
WHAT IS ANANDA?

The reader has already been informed that an actual experiment in cooperative living, known as Ananda World Brotherhood Village, is being carried out by the author and some of his friends in the mountains of Northern California on the basis of the ideas presented in this book.[6] The reader may ask himself, "Why go to all the trouble of starting something myself, when there is a community already flourishing that I might join?"

As a matter of fact, we might be happy for you to reach this conclusion. But please bear in mind that communities, like people, develop distinct characters of their own. To live in a place with a different character from yours might impede your development, even though its essential goals and yours be the same. Many are the roads to truth, and many and varied are the possible applications of broad principles, such as those which have been outlined in these pages.

Ananda presents one such application. Not everyone who reads this book and is attracted to its ideas will feel similarly attracted to the communities I have founded. This is quite as it

---

6 Indeed, as I reread this book many years later, ten Ananda Cooperative Communities have been formed, and are thriving, on three continents. —SK, 2013

should be. The world would be a very dull place indeed if everyone liked and did the same things. The most universal principles must lose some of their universality in actual application, for every such application can only be a limited *example* of the principle itself. Other, and perhaps very different, applications might exemplify it just as truly.

Ananda is a yoga-oriented community. It is dedicated to the search for God and to serving Him through hard, self-purifying work. Our members are disciples, or at least devotees, of Paramhansa Yogananda and of his line of gurus. Most of them are members also of Self-Realization Fellowship, the organization which Yogananda started in this country in 1920. Ananda is not, however, formally affiliated with that or with any other organization.

When Paramhansa Yogananda, during his public lectures in the last years of his life, urged his listeners to band together into "world brotherhood colonies," the general expectation was that his own organization would take the first steps towards forming such a community. But Yogananda was urging his listeners *themselves* to take the initiative. His organization had, and is likely to continue to have, more than it can do already to serve the spiritual demands that are placed upon it by a worldwide and growing interest in yoga. For a community to be successful it is vitally necessary in any case that it run itself; it cannot be supervised effectively from a distance. Its problems will be immediate; they can be solved only by painstaking experiment, not by the remote directives of some larger, but less directly involved, institution.

Ananda is, therefore, completely autonomous.[7]

We are not sectarian in our dealings with the general public, but we find it helpful in our own home environment for our members to be following the same path together.

And what is this path? A few of its highlights are:

A belief in the essential oneness of all religions, and a universal respect for their teachings.

A belief in the value of meditation, and in the spiritual life as the *summum bonum* of human existence.

Respect for the great saints of all religions, who have fulfilled in their own lives the highest spiritual teachings.

A belief that it is insufficient merely to believe—that spiritual truths must be practiced and *experienced* in one's own life, through meditation.

Part II of this book presents the story of our beginnings. The fact that Ananda has been started and is, so far at least, remarkably successful should give hope to others who have wanted to found similar communities, but who have feared that after all the whole idea in this age of business mergers and sprawling urban communities, might prove impracticable.

Some people would rather join an already-working venture. Others would prefer the challenge of starting such a venture themselves. If you do start a cooperative community, I hope you will contact us. We may still be too young ourselves to offer you very much assistance or advice, but it would be

---

7 And each Ananda community (now that we have a number of them) is, for the same reason, completely autonomous. —SK, 2013

good in any case for the cooperative communities in America to become a sort of loose-knit spiritual brotherhood—not formally bound together, but extending to one another that spirit of cooperation which is the basic feature of the cooperative way of life.

EPILOGUE (to Part I)

If you would like to write or phone to Ananda World Brotherhood Village for further information about the community, or about guest programs designed to give one experience of the community, you may do so at:

14618 Tyler Foote Road
Nevada City, California 95959
800-346-5350 or 530-478-7518

For further study on related subjects, I would recommend the following of my books:

The Art of Supportive Leadership gives helpful guidelines to the kind of leadership that is particularly important for the formation of intentional communities.

Education for Life goes deeply into the question of education of children. This book is particularly helpful for people living in intentional communities.

Out of the Labyrinth: For Those Who Want to Believe, But Can't. This book addresses problems raised by the discoveries of modern science, and the impact of those discoveries on traditional values.

PART II:
THE STORY OF ANANDA

Since the sixth edition of this book, Ananda's full name has been changed from Ananda Cooperative Community to Ananda Cooperative Village.

Chapter One
THE EARLY YEARS

Ananda Cooperative Community and Ananda Meditation Retreat are the result of years of intensive work, the cooperation of many friends, faith, and an almost continuous series of miracles.

It all started many years ago, with the study and dreams described in the Introduction to this book. But its more active beginnings date back to 1962. Paradoxically, they first took the form of a search for a place of personal retreat and seclusion for myself.

The religious organization to which I had belonged for fourteen years, and of which I was then the first vice president, on July 28, 1962, dismissed me quite suddenly. My belief in decentralization, wherever possible, as a vital factor in spreading the work had brought me under suspicion of being a potential schismatic.

New doors, as it happened, were being held open for me, but at that time I could see only that every familiar door had been closed. My one desire now was to find a place where I might remain quiet and alone, to pray deeply for new directions.

As everyone knows, it takes money to live in this world. I was offered a post teaching yoga at the American Academy of Asian Studies, in San Francisco, and could not afford to turn it down. Later, I taught at the Cultural Integration Fellowship, also in San Francisco. Gradually, the expense of city living forced me to teach other classes also, on my own. And thus my longing for seclusion, which never left me, was obliged patiently to await its appointed hour.

In the meantime, the number of my new friends was growing steadily.

Through the years between 1962 and 1967, I sought repeatedly for a place of retreat: up and down the coast of Northern California, in the Sierra Nevada, in Arizona. I even made a fruitless journey to Arkansas, and looked at land on the coast of Mexico. I had little money, and did not want to live on someone else's property as a guest. Yet I believed that, if the place presented itself, the means to acquire it would be found also.

The longer I waited, however, the more friends I acquired through my lectures and yoga classes. The thought of seeking a spiritual retreat for myself alone came into increasing conflict with my wish to be of spiritual service to those who depended on me. And so it was that the thought of forming a cooperative community stole up on me once again, as if by a back door. While half of my mind was thinking of finding a place of personal privacy and seclusion, the other half was thinking more and more of a place where others, too, might be able to live a spiritual life together.

All the currents in my life, including especially those since July 1962, in one way or another influenced the formation and development of Ananda Cooperative Community, and helped to determine its special character. Looking back now, I see a pattern in the apparent self-contradiction of wanting a place for seclusion, and at the same time a place where I might build a community. Often, I believe, we are led as it were unconsciously in the direction in which we are meant to go. Even my sudden, and at that time (to me) tragic, severance from the organization to which I had dedicated my life proved at last and in many ways a blessing. At least I can say that if it had not occurred, this book would not have been written, and Ananda would have remained but a dream.

Chapter Two
LAND HO!

It was January 1967. I had not yet found the land I wanted, but the income for it was suddenly beginning to materialize. The Peace Corps had offered me a well-paying job for a semester at the University of California at Davis. (I was to teach a group of volunteers all about Indian culture and civilization, but my approach began with Indian philosophy, and this proved too much for them. They wanted, they said, to learn about *India,* not about Indian philosophy. So I brought in outside teachers to tell them about five-year plans, and—on their insistence—about the Negro question in America.) In addition, I had begun charging for my yoga classes—reluctantly at first, because I look upon teaching as a form of service, and had therefore been simply letting people donate as they could, or as they chose. I had come to find, however, that for many students the absence of a fee tends to make their attendance and personal practice more-or-less casual. At last I was persuaded to set a fee, though at the same time I determined not to exclude sincere-seeming students who could not afford to pay it. The plan worked well: There was a remarkable increase in the seriousness of the students, and a sudden spurt also in my income.

I had a feeling that I would soon be needing this extra money.

I was right. Until this time, I had been content to live marginally, barely raising the money each month to pay the rent on my apartment. But the time was fast approaching when I would take the first definite steps toward developing what was to become known as Ananda.

The income I derived from the Peace Corps job enabled me to publish my first books: *Yours—the Universe!*, *Yoga Postures for Self-Awareness*, and *The Book of Bhrigu* (a report on an ancient Indian book of prophecy). With these publications I set up the first business by which I hoped the cooperative community, once I had founded it, would support itself.

Jeannie Campbell, the receptionist and general secretary for the print shop where two of these books were being printed, was a devout Zen Buddhist. We had many lively discussions on the differences between Zen and yoga. She also gave me a running description of the development of Tassajara, a Zen Buddhist retreat that was being built in the mountains near Carmel, California, and a place with which she was closely connected.

During the course of one of these conversations, I told her of my wish to find some land for a retreat of my own.

"Say," she cried, "why don't you contact Dick Baker? He's the president of the Zen Center here in San Francisco, and he's in charge of building Tassajara. If anyone would know about available land, he would."

I dutifully jotted his name down, but never got around to

phoning him. In my long experience of "leads" that had led nowhere, this one seemed simply another improbability.

A week or two later, however, I was in a small shop in San Francisco, and was obliged to wait while another customer was being served. This person was speaking of some land that he and some friends were thinking of buying for a retreat. Unable to resist the entree, I mentioned that I was looking for something similar myself. During the course of a still-casual conversation, he pulled out a map of his proposed property and spread it out on a table, adding that he still needed a few people to buy into the property with him.

Had this looked like an ordinary real estate deal, I might not have been quite so intrigued, but he wanted the land for a spiritual retreat. This was definitely intriguing. As a person, too, I found him attractive. "What is your name?" I asked.

"Dick Baker."

The very person Jeannie had urged me to look up! As Dick explained it to me later, when the appeal went out to raise the money for the purchase of Tassajara, the sum involved was so high that it drew a number of alternate offers from friends and sympathizers. These persons wrote to say, in effect, "If you find that you can't raise that much money, I have some land that I'd be willing to sell you at a very low price because of the spiritual purpose involved."

Partly to check out possible alternatives to Tassajara, and partly because he also wanted a place of retreat for himself and his family, Dick Baker had visited all of the proposed places.

Of them all, his favorite was a tract of 172 acres in the foothills of the Sierra Nevada, near Nevada City, California. It was only $250 an acre—inexpensive for California, in fact only half the usual price of land even in this remote area. But it was more money than Dick personally could afford. He decided, therefore, to try to get six of his friends to purchase the land with him, each of them receiving twenty-four acres. Somehow the idea, and Dick Baker himself, felt completely "right" to me. I asked him if I might accompany him on his next trip up there. He said he was planning one in the early spring, and that he would be glad for me to come along.

When we went up, it was with two of his friends, Allen Ginsberg and Gary Snyder, both well-known poets, and both interested in buying twenty-four-acre parcels for themselves. A woman writer accompanied us, too; she was working on an article about Allen for *The New Yorker.*

Our trip took us far out into the countryside. The last three miles were dirt road, deeply rutted and barely passable after the winter rains. The altitude was three thousand feet. The air was fresh. The property was rolling, wooded, serene, and gave onto several beautiful views of distant snowcapped mountains. I went off in one direction by myself. Gary went in another. We were "feeling" the land.

The impression came to me strongly that my Gurus had already blessed the particular section of the land to which I had felt drawn. It was an eastern exposure, and to me, as a yogi, especially attractive. Would the others want it too? If it came to a conflict of interests, I knew that, as the latecomer to the group, I was the last in line to choose.

But amazingly, each of us felt drawn to a different section of the property. I could not help feeling that it was for this place that God had made me wait all those years. At last my search was ended.

But I little knew what struggles had just begun!

Chapter Three
MY FIRST NON-HOME

Somehow I find that I have always lived my life on two levels: a conscious level, on which I approach things according to my own personal inclinations; and another one, more dimly perceived, on which I seem to know how things are going to have to be whether I want them that way or not. My experience of being dismissed in 1962 came as a complete shock on one level; on another, although no warning had been given, it was expected long in advance.

An example of this curious duality of awareness concerns another case where one level pitted itself against the other. In the latter months of 1963 I was staying on a ranch in Arizona. At that time I was hoping that I might support myself by writing, and was determined if possible to avoid all public activity.

I received a letter in November from Dr. Haridas Chaudhuri, the founder-director of Cultural Integration Fellowship in San Francisco, inviting me to give a series of classes in his ashram that winter. I wrote back explaining my anxiety to stay out of the public eye. Yet I knew with a puzzling inner certainty that I would be not only teaching in his ashram that winter, but living in it.

I returned to the San Francisco Bay Area to be with my parents for Christmas. Shortly afterward I was invited to attend a quiet Saturday evening dinner at which Dr. Chaudhuri and his wife also were guests. My scheduled departure for Arizona was only four days away. My inner certainty of an unscheduled change, however, had prevented me from even thinking about packing. At the end of the evening, the Chaudhuris bade me a safe journey. There was something about our parting that was unreal.

The next morning, in the middle of his Sunday sermon, Dr. Chaudhuri fell over with a heart attack and was rushed in a critical condition to the hospital. He had no one to take his place at the ashram. As his friend, I knew I had no choice but to offer my services during the long months it would take him to recuperate.

In a similar manner I knew, when I first bought the land for my retreat, that I would not be permitted to enjoy it until I had founded a community as well. I wanted in any case to share the retreat with a few others as temporary guests, or as permanent hermits. But the community that I felt I was being directed to form was a busy place for families with children, self-supportive industries—in short, a place such as I have described in the first part of this book.

What about my long-desired seclusion? The community, I decided, would have to wait. The retreat for others would have to wait. First I would have my own place. Everything else could develop gradually, if it was meant to, out of this first step. I should have listened to that soft inner whisper. It told me from the start that I had made the wrong choice, and that if the other ventures were to develop in the right way, I would have to think of myself last, not first.

"But all I want," I told myself, "is a place to seek God. What's so selfish about that?" If I'd waited for an answer, the rest of that year might have gone more smoothly for me.

As a structure for my home, I had decided if possible to build a dome. The idea had first come to me in India, in 1961. There I had planned to build a temple, and my meditations had suggested this type of structure to my mind as the most conducive to inner calmness and expansion. What I envisioned was a hemisphere coming down on all sides to about eye level—more or less like the inside of a planetarium. A flat ceiling, it seemed to me, had the psychological, perhaps even psychic, effect of pressing down on the head. An arched ceiling seemed to invite aspiration, but more in the form of external than of internal worship. The high domes that one finds in some temples around the world suggest a heavenly state far removed from any present human expectations. For meditation, with the inner peace that it brings to the soul even in the present life, the sort of dome I envisioned seemed ideal. It harmonized with nature herself, with her round "inverted bowl" of the sky. The human head, too, is a dome; perhaps the rays of energy going outward from the brain are echoed back most harmoniously from the inner surface of a similar structure. After returning from India I visited a planetarium, and was interested to discover that even with children squirming and giggling all around me, and while people were still entering and the lights were still on, a distinct impression of peace emanated from that interior.

I wanted, as I say, to construct a perfect dome. But inquiries convinced me that the cost would be prohibitive. One day, Karen Leffler, a student in one of my classes, introduced me to a concept that was new to me: the geodesic dome, an invention by Buckminster Fuller. For me, it was a compromise. His straight lines and flat planes produce a marvel of engineering, but esthetically they conflict with the roundness of a true hemisphere. Still, it was the closest thing to a possibility that I had come upon so far. I resolved to follow in the footsteps of Buckminster Fuller.

It was easier resolved than done. No one seemed to know the mathematical formula. One company that I found made domes, but were tool designers, not artists; their squat structures looked to me like toadstools out of a book of nursery rhymes. This, I decided, was just too much of a compromise.

At last Charles Tart, a professor at U.C. Davis, showed me a geodesic dome that he was constructing in his back yard. It was called a "sun dome." Inexpensive, beautiful in its simplicity, and easy for an amateur like me to construct, it offered me my first ray of real hope. I clutched it as eagerly (and as foolishly) as a drowning man would a straw.

Easy it may have been to construct, but building the platform, cutting the struts exactly to the required angles, assembling them into triangles, then covering them with plastic, required months of unceasing labor. After all my years of waiting, I was determined to build my retreat if possible this year.

No, Kriyananda, it was not to be. I got the dome up all right. The last triangle was about to go in, after which, supposedly, the dome would stand firm. But until it had been fully assembled, its strength was precarious.

Suddenly a strong gust of wind rushed up from the valley; the entire structure fell to the ground, a jumble of matchsticks and plastic.

Refusing to give up, I set out immediately to replace the broken pieces, reassembling all the triangles, and stapling them together with greater care than the first time. Weeks later, the new structure was up. It was, in all fairness, more beautiful than anything we have built since. Its delicate struts were an esthetic delight. But Keats was wrong: Beauty is not necessarily truth. The "sun dome" proved a snare and a delusion.

I did not realize that the planners had designed it to sit cozily in a fenced-in back yard, as Charlie Tart's was, well protected from strong winds, and preferably even from the mildest zephyr. Up on the hilltop at Ananda the late autumn winds can get up to sixty or seventy miles an hour. In the first storm we had, my beautiful dome-house simply disintegrated. I walked away from it without even looking back.

But after a few days I summoned the courage to try once again. This time, after re-cutting many more pieces and reassembling them, I screwed them all firmly together with large metal plates. This time, I was sure, no wind could possibly rip them apart.

The wind didn't have to. Alas, I knew nothing of its power to lift a hemisphere, similarly to the lift it exerts on the upper portion of the wing of an airplane. I returned to Ananda soon after I had put up my dome for the third time. I was eager, before winter descended in earnest, to get at least a little of that solitary meditation I had been planning for so long.

I arrived to find pieces of the dome draped artistically over the surrounding bushes. Worst of all, because this time the pieces had been screwed so firmly together, virtually every one of them was broken. There was nothing to do but recognize defeat, and accept it calmly. I sat down on the open platform, and, surprisingly perhaps, had a joyous meditation.

But to me it was a sign that I would not be able to have my own home until I had built a temple, and perhaps even a community, for the benefit of others.

Chapter Four
ANANDA MEDITATION RETREAT

My home-to-be had blown down for the third time. I found myself almost without funds. There was no choice for me but to go back to teaching classes again. This I did intensively, traveling to a different city every evening, determined now to raise the money necessary to build a retreat for others as well as for myself. And as long as I was putting forth so much energy, I decided if possible also to take the first steps toward building the cooperative community I had been contemplating.

To many people, my dream of starting a community, and at the same time of spending a long time in seclusion, must have seemed absurdly self-contradictory. But I knew now that it was not so much a question of what *I* wanted, but of what God wanted for me. And somehow an inner intuition assured me that the two things *would* be possible.

For nothing within me responded to the idea of *managing* a cooperative community. I knew that if I, as the founder, took up the task of administrating its affairs, and of personally guaranteeing its success, I would have to write off the next twenty-five years of my life to developing this project alone. My task, I felt, was rather to devote my energies, and such experience as

I might be able to claim, to helping *others* to form a community. I might serve it thereafter, if the members so wished, as a spiritual director, but definitely not as a business manager. If I could adhere to the single role of spiritual counselor, it seemed to me that seclusion much of the time would actually help me in that work.

There was another factor influencing my decision to begin now, rather than later, to develop the community. It was the feeling, in a positive sense, that there might not be very much time left to get it going. When large masses of people speak of sensing an impending cataclysm, one cannot but feel that something serious may well be in the air. I was conscious also of my own corroborative feelings in the matter, and especially of the many dire warnings of my Guru.

A busy community of families, self-supportive industries, and crying babies would have ruined the meditative calm of the retreat. It would have betrayed not only my personal hopes, but also the condition on which Dick Baker had been kind enough to let me buy into the property. None of the others was planning to build there for at least two years, however. Nor did I see how, in my present role as a fundraiser, I could hope to get any seclusion sooner than that. A strong sense that the community was destined to be gave me confidence that, if we started it at the Retreat, it would soon be strong enough to move onto land of its own.

There was another factor influencing the direction of my thinking. Two twenty-four-acre parcels adjoining mine had not yet been sold. It was already late in January 1968, and, according to our agreement with the sellers, if all seven of the parcels were not sold by April 1 of that year the entire sale would fall through. Dick was confident that he would find the extra buyers, but so far, in ten out of thirteen months, only we, the original four, had bought land there. I was not quite so confident that three more people would come forward in the remaining two months to save the situation.

I phoned Dick and told him that I might be able to buy the two parcels next to mine. "But please understand," I said, "that I would not buy this land only for my own retreat. For that, twenty-four acres are quite enough." I went on to describe my community idea, and to assure him that the use of these extra acres for that purpose would be only temporary. It was asking a lot of him to believe that I would really be in a position to move the community away in two or three years (I believe we set the maximum limit at five years), but he must have caught some of my conviction, for he agreed.

For years an old friend of mine, Oleta Burger, had been offering to give me money to help start a community. Repeatedly I had put her off, wanting to test the sincerity of her offer. I now told her that I thought the time was right, and asked if she was still interested. She was. In this way the two extra parcels at the Retreat were acquired, bringing our total number of acres to seventy-two.

Soon afterwards I called the first formal meeting to discuss plans for forming a cooperative community. I had planned to have only a few close friends and coworkers at this first meeting. Others, however, whom I hardly knew, but who claimed to be interested in the project, appeared also, uninvited. Their presence proved a mixed blessing.

"How do we know you're on the level?" one of them demanded.

"If you start something this big, you'll soon forget all about your ideal of serving people."

"I know a teacher from India who became involved in building a place similar to this. It took so much of his energy that he lost his inner peace, and today he's a MONSTER!"

"Think of it, everyone. If Kriyananda really wanted to draw us into this thing as partners, *why didn't he call this meeting sooner?*"

The only thing to do at this point was to serve tea and cookies.

But the meeting was not a total disaster. Realizing that by mere talk I would never be able to give people a clear picture of what I had in mind, I sat down at last with the gathered notes and reflections of many years, and wrote this book. After publishing it in loose-leaf form, and distributing it to all who expressed an interest in the idea, I decided to give everyone time to reflect on it before broaching the subject again.

My own enthusiasm had led me to expect a quick, positive response from anyone to whom I described my ideas. I had overlooked the many years it had taken me to grow into these ideas myself.

Many potentially interested persons, I now realized, needed not only enough time to reflect on these ideas, but also the reassurance of seeing something already solidly accomplished. It is one of the curious facts of human life that, for most ventures to be started, people are the prime necessity, but that, for most people to become involved at all, the venture itself must already be well under way.

No one, I decided, could accuse me of black motives if I built a meditation retreat. It was a project about which little theorizing was necessary, and it would attract active participation. Slowly, out of this group labor, the seeds were to sprout that would grow in time to become the cooperative community.

I had reached the conclusion, by means which the charitable reader will doubtless fail to recognize, that I was not cut out to be a carpenter. The worst of it was that none of my friends were carpenters, either. But by this time I was making a fair amount of money teaching classes. Some money was coming in also from generous friends. This income, plus some stocks that my father had given me over the years, totaled about sixteen thousand dollars—enough for me to think of hiring professional help.

I still wanted those geodesic domes. The only company that made them was still that one which manufactured prefabs vaguely reminiscent of toadstools. I bowed to the inevitable. At least these were something I could afford.

I found a carpenter who expressed confidence that he would be able to put up our buildings in two weeks. "Go ahead," I told him. Had I shared his experience in construction, I doubt that I would have shared his confidence.

The first thing the carpenter (now the foreman) wanted was a couple of professional helpers. A number of my friends worked with him, too, at greatly reduced wages, glad (I hope) of the chance to spend a summer out of doors in the woods. In these ways wages soared to $1,000 a week. But the worst news was still to come. After two weeks, around the middle of July 1968, not even the foundations had been finished. In all, the project was to take two and a half months. Long before that time, I ran out of money.

No problem, I told myself. The bank would surely lend me what I needed.

But they wouldn't. Their reasoning went something like this: So I was making money by teaching yoga; so, maybe a few people were crazy enough to study this absurd "science," but after all, one can't fool all the people all of the time; the yoga fad was bound to pass, and, if one was to have any faith in human nature at all, one surely couldn't expect such madness to last out the year.

For me, their rejection was a major blow. We had a temple, a common dome (kitchen, dining room, and living room), bathhouse, office, and my home all under construction, and it was imperative that they be finished before the winter storms ruined them. But the next thing I knew, the foreman and one of his two professional helpers had walked off the job. The third carpenter remained loyal, but we still had bills outstanding that amounted to thousands of dollars. Only to complete the construction was to cost me at least another $12,000. I was just screwing up my courage to try to raise this amount when the local lumber company placed a lien on the land. (So now I learned what a lien was! Years in a monastery had not prepared me for certain things.)

I persuaded my various creditors to accept partial monthly payments. My past record of prompt payment was an advantage. Even so, however, the least that I was able to get them to accept totaled $2,500 a month, for five months. In addition to this sum I had all my other normal expenses: apartment, car, books and correspondence office, classes, food, etc. My years in a monastery had not prepared me for this, either!

Or had they? Knowledgeable effort alone could not possibly have taken me over this hurdle. The only thing that seems to work in times of real crisis is faith in God. I plunged in, doing the best I could, and placed the outcome wholly in His hands.

More students than ever enrolled in the classes. Friends helped generously, even nobly. Every month, several times with very little to spare, my commitments of $2,500 were paid, and all my other expenses were met. At one point the lumber company, which I had been paying regularly according to our agreement, tried anyway to force a foreclosure. Miraculously, my income that month was greater than usual; I paid off the entire debt, and was left, after paying my other bills, with $1.37 in my bank account!

By the end of the year, the retreat had been not only built, but very nearly paid off. People were beginning to "rally round the flag." It was time to begin thinking seriously once again about forming our cooperative community.

Chapter Five
THE PURCHASE OF ANANDA FARM

As early as the end of 1967 a friend had volunteered to stay at Ananda and act as caretaker. By late summer 1968, we were holding our first retreats in the barely completed buildings. Through the winter of that year several persons were already living at the Retreat as hermits.

It was in February 1969 that we held our second meeting in San Francisco to discuss forming a community. By this time, interest and confidence in the venture had grown strong. The question was no longer whether, but *how,* to begin. The decisions reached in that second meeting, and in others that followed shortly after it, have had to be altered to a large extent as experience has taught us greater wisdom. But a start was at least made then, and by the spring of 1969 the first families began arriving at Ananda.

Our plan, as I have already said, was only to *start* the family aspect of the community at the Retreat, and after a couple of years or so, when we had grown stronger, to buy land for it elsewhere—perhaps, I thought, in the area of Auburn, fifty miles to the south, where the planting season is longer.

God had other plans for us, however, and to set our minds

thinking in the right direction He sent us some particularly noisy children at the very outset. Meditations in the temple became a backdrop of silent disapproval to gleeful shouts, angry accusations, and bitter tears over which no one had the slightest control. Auburn was too far away for such a fledgling community. I began wondering whether suitable land might not be found nearby—and soon.

Dick Baker at this time became worried that we might not, despite the best of intentions, be strong enough within two years or so to move the families away from the Retreat. After all, my assurances were based on *my* faith, not on his. And so it happened that just now, when we were on the point of starting our cooperative community in earnest, and were at last completely out of debt, I received a letter from Dick asking me to undertake no further construction until we could meet and discuss things in person. Unfortunately, he was in Japan, and was not expected to return until autumn. It was still only June. His request seemed catastrophic.

In fact, however, it proved a real blessing.

I received his letter on a Friday morning. That afternoon I drove up to Ananda from my San Francisco apartment, and stopped off in Sacramento on the way to visit a friend of mine, Dr. Gordon Runnels, in his office. While I was there another friend of his, a real estate agent, stopped by, and began speaking excitedly about what he called "the hottest land buy I've ever seen." I asked him where it was. He replied, "In the hills north of Auburn."

And where north of Auburn? He drew out a map to show me. It was of our area! The acreage he was pointing to, in fact, was located only a few minutes' drive from Ananda Retreat.

"The owner," he told me, "is a terminal cancer patient. He wants to settle his affairs as quickly as possible. His land has been subdivided, mostly into forty-acre parcels. It isn't even on the market yet, but already the guys in the office are beginning to place options on pieces of it for themselves, and are getting their friends interested."

"I'm going up very near there this afternoon," I told him. "Would you like to come along and show me this land?"

So it was that, in the fading daylight, we found ourselves walking over some of the most beautiful countryside I have ever seen in my life—a life that has taken me twice around the world, and to some forty different countries.

"Would you be able," I asked him, "to hold a few pieces for me over the weekend?" I mentioned which pieces, specifically, I wanted; they amounted to most of the property.

"I'll try," he replied.

The down payment for the parcels that I wanted came to $13,500—an unthinkably high sum for which to raise even promises over one weekend. "But," I said, "if God wants us to have it, He should have no problem working things out for us."

It has never been my good fortune to attract wealthy sponsors, perhaps because of a deep-seated fear of being owned. But I know many people, and a few of them have at least *some* money. I got busy on the telephone. By Saturday morning, less than twenty-four hours after receiving Dick Baker's discouraging letter, I had promises of loans and gifts totaling exactly $13,500.

"To play it safe," the real estate agent told me Saturday morning when I phoned him, "I went into the office at two o'clock last night. It's lucky that I did so. I was able to reserve all the parcels you wanted, but this morning five or six of the other fellows came and pleaded with me to let them have some of your parcels. By getting those promises of help so quickly, you've acted just in time, I can tell you. What you've done is snatch that land right out from everyone else's noses."

There was still the matter of talking over this purchase with our present members. They all agreed, however, that it was the only possible step to take at this time. And so it was that we acquired well over two hundred acres of additional land for our families, farming, and heavier industries. This new land became known as Ananda Farm. It is only six miles from Ananda Meditation Retreat—close enough to have remained a part of the same community.

Interestingly, almost all of the original promises of money for the down payment fell through. We needed the initial confidence which those promises gave us, but God had other ways of raising the down payment when it actually came due.

The story of the farm purchase had a particularly poignant ending. It had saddened me to think that our good fortune was coming to us at the cost of the former owner's life. Sometime later I met his doctor, who happens to have married the daughter of some friends of my family when we lived in Scarsdale, New York. He told me that this man's cancer, which had indeed been terminal, had been quite marvelously cured not long after we had taken possession of the land.

Chapter Six
COMMUNAL BEGINNINGS

Ananda Cooperative Community really started, at least in its present form, with the purchase of Ananda Farm. It began with an explosion which we very nearly didn't survive.

The news spread by an amazingly efficient underground grapevine that a new "commune" had been started and needed members. People began arriving from everywhere. One afternoon alone there were seven cars in our driveway, full of people wanting to join Ananda. Many of this horde were the usual dropouts—seekers, not for a positive way of life, but for a soft berth. They ate our food, ran up our phone bill, and told us how we ought to be living. Most of them required our time and attention. A few of them, of course, we actually wanted with us as members.

For of course we did need members. What we didn't need was an invasion. We had to get the word out as quickly as possible by the ever-efficient grapevine that Ananda was not at all "where it's at." It took awhile, but we were relieved at last to find ourselves being dubbed in certain circles as "uptight," materialistic, not a real "commune." And in other circles, we were grateful to learn, people were beginning to think of us as dedicated, responsible, sincere. In short, Ananda began to develop its own "image"; increasingly, those who came even as visitors were to be those who were in tune with us.

Perhaps my own greatest struggle in the beginning stemmed from the fact that we had to admit enough members to make the Farm economically possible. Many of these newcomers were people who had no knowledge of the background of Ananda, nor any special desire to help me, as its founder, to fulfill my dreams for it. Their attitude was perfectly understandable. A basic principle on which the community had been founded, in fact, was that no member would have more than one vote. That, of course, included me. It was important for me to adhere to this principle if I didn't want Ananda to turn into a dictatorship.

Yet it was also true that I had spent years growing into ideas that most of these newcomers had never even considered before. Many of my so-called dreams for Ananda were, I at least knew, essential to its very survival. Others were necessary to my own continued interest in the community. In addition to wanting to impress upon our members certain ideas that I knew to be vital to its success and future growth, I wanted to educate them to the thought of accepting real responsibility for managing their own affairs. For I had determined from the start to stick to my original notion of not becoming the community's manager.

Partly by working personally with those members who showed a willingness to assume definite responsibility, partly by offering sound enough reasons for my proposals, and partly by laying constant stress on our spiritual directions, I was able in time to accomplish my objectives. More and more, the community took on the character I had dreamed of in founding it, even to managing its own affairs in an admirable and responsible manner.

One of our first struggles was over the question of drugs, which every newcomer to the community had promised not to take, but which soon began to exercise an attraction again for certain people, especially when things became outwardly difficult. There were a couple of times when I had to be firm, even to asking one person to leave, but on the whole I felt that reason, and a growing spiritual force in the community, would solve the problem for us. Eventually my expectations proved justified.

Another problem was one of the community's self-identity. Many of the members wanted, or at least expected, Ananda to develop as a close-knit family unit, a sort of "tribe." Gradually, however, our people came to experience for themselves the truth, which I have stressed in this book, that a fair measure of privacy is spiritually desirable, as well as conducive to communal harmony. Thus, without very much difficulty, the community decided on its own that it wanted to become more what this book suggests, an intentional village, rather than a typical "commune."

When we first moved to Ananda, so our neighbors later told us, word quickly spread through the surrounding community that "bad news" had come to Nevada County. But we came wishing to become responsible citizens and good neighbors. Soon the general impression changed. People found that we respected local laws and authorities, paid our bills promptly, and added a certain positive aura of our own to the area. A surprisingly large number of people, moreover, though not members of our community, have moved to Nevada County as a direct consequence of our being here. All in all, Ananda has been good for local business. The good will that we have received from the surrounding community stands in sharp contrast to the local hostility that a number of other communities have encountered.

Much more remarkable than harmony with people outside the community is the harmony of the members within it. Very rarely now is there any friction among them. Part of the reason for this, certainly, is that our members are men and women of good will. Yet even people of good will have been known not to get along well together. I think it must be added, therefore, that our members are developing, through their daily meditations, a spiritual maturity which puts their relations with one another on a higher plane.

This growing spiritual maturity reflects itself in their management of community affairs. It is the greatest single reason why, despite Ananda's chaotic beginnings, its direction of growth has been steadily toward greater harmony, cooperation, and a sense of true spiritual kinship.

Chapter Seven
FINANCIAL PROBLEMS

The history of Ananda from its inception has, alas, been intimately connected with a struggle over finances. Our purchase of the farm meant an assumption of payments in the amount of $1,750 a month—in direct contradiction to my own advice in this book that new communities try to stay out of debt. But we really had no other choice. And my experiences so far had given me some reason for believing that God would continue to open the way for us, whenever He limited our choices as strictly as He had this time.

Again and again in my life God has shown me that the greatest calamities, if accepted with faith in Him, are the very doorway through which He chooses to send His greatest blessings. Either He has a very twisted sense of humor, or this is His way of developing our faith! For faith is a dynamic thing. It must be *exercised;* it cannot be merely entertained, like some pleasing sentiment. (It should be added, however, that one's exercise of it must be commensurate with one's actual experience of its powers. Otherwise it will become mere presumption, and will usually be ineffectual.)

The mortgage payments, a heavy burden at first, proved

in time to be one of the principal and most necessary factors in drawing the community together. For money was, at the beginning, a bad word to most of our members. It spelled materialism, ego, worldliness—everything that we were trying to outgrow. Many of our people had yet to learn that lethargy, too, is a form of materialism—far worse so, in fact, than money madness; that a nonproductive life is destructive to spiritual consciousness; and that money is only a form of energy: It can be used wisely, as well as misused. As I consider the (for me) immense amounts of money that I had to make or raise in getting Ananda started, I am continually astonished at the fact that my real gain from those painful struggles has been inward, not outward. To work hard to materialize a high ideal is not materialism. God had given us Ananda Farm with a strict condition attached to it. If we wanted to hang onto our blessing, we had to work hard to pay for it. A growing love for the community and for our environment induced the members to begin to work earnestly at various self-supportive industries. Gradually, they came to discover that their work was a valid form of service, and as such a source of great inner blessings for themselves.

It took a while to develop this understanding. I moved to Ananda in June 1969. My fond expectation was that many people working together would free me of the need to be out in the cities all the time teaching yoga classes. But at first people simply did not work together. In fact, some of them didn't even work. And those who did work, and hard, could not generate any real income at the very outset; it takes time to establish a profitable business.

Things were coming together, if slowly. They only hadn't "clicked" yet. But there was a time, towards the end of 1969, when everything came close to disintegrating completely. Winter was coming, and most of our people didn't know how they would face it. The mortgage payments had been deferred because the sellers had not yet put in certain roads which they had promised us. Suddenly we received notices of intent to foreclose. Few of our members could even think in terms of such large sums of money. Drugs became an escape for some of them. People retreated into a kind of fantasy world with regard to the mortgage: If God wanted it paid, *He* would take care of it. This was certainly the bleakest period in our history.

I decided to give some people time to come to grips with reality, and others time to get their industries going. I had no intention of spending my life working away from Ananda just so that others might live there and play. It was particularly trying to me to find that a few people saw in my willingness to work for them the very justification for their own faith that God would, somehow, take care of them. I agreed to assume the responsibility for paying the mortgage only through May 1970. Thus, I lived in Sacramento through the winter months, teaching classes again.

The hardest blow for me came when, after paying regularly on the mortgage for four months, I received a notice that if within two weeks I didn't pay, in addition, all those back payments, the property would be foreclosed. I had thought we would win a waiver on the grounds that the sellers had not fulfilled their promises. I was powerless, however, to force my point. In two weeks, in other words, I had to come up with an *additional* $4,500 or we'd lose the whole Farm.

"Face it," a friend of mine said the evening that I received this letter, "you can't win 'em all."

"Come on over to my place," another friend urged me, "and have some tea. It will make you feel better."

"What do you mean?" I cried. "I'm not interested in how I *feel* about this! I'm interested in what I can *do* about it!"

I probably looked stunned; I certainly felt it. But the right time to console oneself with feelings of nonattachment is certainly not during the thick of a battle. So long as even half a day still remained, I had at least a chance to succeed. In fact, I was inwardly certain of success.

When I returned home that night, I began making a round of urgent telephone calls. I managed to defer the foreclosure a month and a half longer. The final payment to forestall it was due June 1. With God's grace, I paid it, along with the regular mortgage payment for that month, on May 31.

I then moved back to Ananda, and turned the responsibility for further mortgage payments over to the entire community.

The members in the meantime had grown spiritually, as well as in a practical sense. I returned to find the morale high, the industries promising, and the love for our way of life now strong enough for people to want to make the sacrifices necessary to preserve it.

For myself, I must admit that I had reached a point of exhaustion. For the remainder of that summer it was all I could do to give retreat classes. After years of fundraising activities, the time had come, I felt, for me to go more deeply into myself.

A spur in this direction came a month after my return to Ananda. In the early morning hours of July 3, our Retreat temple burned down. It was uninsured; the loss to us was considerable.

But again there were fortunate consequences. We all need a few hardships in life to encourage us to strengthen our grip on positive attitudes. In that sense, this was a golden opportunity. Later that day a couple of us entered a nearby grocery store.

"You are singing!" exclaimed the proprietress, a French woman. "When our house burn down last year, six months I cry and cry!"

But after all, why *not* sing? To identify one's happiness with mere things is to live in bondage. The loss of the temple, in fact, brought me inner blessings that went far beyond any personal determination to keep "a stiff upper lip." I felt a deep inner reassurance, and a stronger conviction than ever that nothing in life matters except serving and pleasing God. From now on, too, I knew that God wanted me to work more intensively on building my own, inner "temple."

The labor of rebuilding the temple, and the affirmation of courage that it entailed, helped substantially to bring our people together. This loss in fact, like many other hardships, in time proved a real blessing. We had new members by now who were familiar with the problems of constructing geodesic domes. The new temple is larger and much more beautiful than the first.

These last nine years have been a struggle. But as I tell people, even if, after all these efforts, Ananda were to fail, I would feel that I had gained permanent benefits from all this work. Outward things come and go. Worldly success and failure are inextricably bound to each other. The gains that are lasting are within. Ultimately, they are the sole reason for all our outward labors.

As for me, increasingly since the temple burned down I have entered a life of seclusion. For months now, in fact, I have been coming out only on weekends to speak. As it has turned out, my seclusion has proved more helpful to Ananda than my strenuous efforts fundraising ever did, and has also given people incentive to work harder so as to make it possible for me to remain here full time.

Chapter Eight
LESSONS LEARNED

Many are the lessons that these past years have taught me. In a sense, what I have learned seems too personal to have included among the suggestions in the first part of this book. But they may be useful to some readers who want to follow the same route of starting a community. Let us therefore consider a few of these lessons here.

My first suggestion would be: Be prepared for hardships and difficulties. Perhaps I am only projecting. Ananda was born out of hardship. I would like to think that our experience, in this respect at least, has been uniquely our own. I rather doubt it, however. And on the plus side I have learned that divine grace grows in the soil of hearts that have been softened by suffering.

People often tend to give up after a few hardships. If they have some faith in God, they will often say, "These obstacles prove that He doesn't want me to go in this direction." Well, they may or they may not prove it. If you see ample signs of His support in other ways, or if you feel inwardly sure of His support, obstacles and hardships may actually be marks of His favor, of His desire to help you to grow strong. The important thing is *not to be afraid* to sacrifice for the things in life that are worthwhile to you. Triumph always implies a struggle. Life's easy satisfactions bring us no inner growth, and soon prove stultifying to the soul.

The thrice-repeated loss of my first geodesic dome, which was to be my own home, taught me a lesson that I think may prove helpful to others who want to start communities: Build for others first, and only then for yourself.

The opposition that I encountered when I first proposed the actual formation of a cooperative community forced me to follow a line of approach that I think might also prove helpful to others. Whatever the central aim of your community is to be, I suggest that you build first with a view to focusing the community's consciousness there. In our case, since our ideal was spiritual growth, the fact of having a temple first was vital to our future development.

Essential to our own development also was the publication of this book, for it gave everyone a chance to see and to understand where we were headed. If you propose to use this book as a basis for a community of your own, it would help you to insist that all your prospective members study it, if only to help them to arrive at a clearer consensus concerning the directions they themselves want to go.

I have always felt that one reason God made it possible for me to meet all my financial obligations, some of which were so staggering (during most of my adult life, my allowance, as a monk, had been only twenty dollars a month!), was that I never allowed the severest pressures to tempt me to think of getting from people, rather than giving to them. If they couldn't afford to take my classes, I let them attend anyway in exchange for some simple service, such as setting up the room for a class, or spending a weekend working at Ananda. Some people took advantage of my leniency, but I knew that it was God, not man, from whom my help was really coming. I believe that others would find it helpful, similarly, to place service first at *all* times, and not to think that a good cause justifies a temporary consciousness of greed.

One mistake I made in trying to interest people in Ananda was to present them at the outset with too sweeping a plan. Most people require time to grow into a new idea. Indeed, probably most people are never as stirred by the thought of a challenge as the kind of person who goes about starting things. If you want to start a community, therefore, you would probably do well not to let the presentation of your vision get too far ahead of the actual situation at hand. One step at a time is the safest policy.

Our direction of development at Ananda has several times forced us to take steps that are in opposition to some of the recommendations in this book. We assumed a heavy debt, for example, when we acquired Ananda Farm, though I've recommended that no new community do so. We abandoned from the outset an idea that I proposed in earlier editions of this book, namely, that the community be the sole employer; and another, taken from B.F. Skinner's *Walden Two,* that workers be paid at least partly in the form of negotiable chits, rather than in cash. Both ideas proved more cumbersome than useful. It wasn't long, in fact, before we decided to adopt the system we had all grown up with and understood: to have separate, privately owned industries, and to let other people work in them for pay.

In the early editions of this book I suggested selling shares in the community as a means of developing it. This has proved unfeasible for us, and indeed I no longer recommend it for others.

We have made changes also in our setup of the governing body. What appears now in this book in the chapter on government is substantially the system we now follow, but in earlier editions I suggested something more elaborate—much *too* elaborate for a group of people whose main wish in living together is to live simply.

People often ask us how we have been so successful, particularly when so many similar communities have fallen apart. Many reasons might be advanced, but I think of these the most important are three: 1) We find our peace inwardly first, in meditation, and only secondarily from one another; 2) we have learned that the secret of work is joyous service; and 3) we have learned that to see God in one another, and in all men, is to dissolve all sense of differences between us and them. People are often astonished at how little friction there is here. But there is really no mystery about that. Inner peace, like an oil, keeps the machinery of life flowing smoothly, all its parts working together harmoniously.

People sometimes ask us, What about our plans for the future? How large do we want to grow? What responsibility do we feel toward the cooperative community movement as a whole? Do we hope to open branches of Ananda Cooperative Community elsewhere?

Our plans for the future include a spiritually oriented "How-to-Live" school, patterned after the ideas in this book, and as much as possible the educational ideals of our Guru, Paramhansa Yogananda. The school will begin as a secondary school, open to children from outside the community. It will be situated on fifteen acres of land that we have acquired for this purpose, adjacent to, and yet (because of the topography) separate from the Farm property. I refer to this as a future project because we have as yet constructed no buildings for the school, but in fact, in spite of this minor handicap, we do already have a small high school, complete with accredited teachers, operating for the time being at Ananda Retreat. Students from outside the community live in retreat cabins, which are less in demand by retreatants during the cooler months of the year. We plan to place the school under The Yoga Fellowship, a nonprofit religious corporation that I founded in 1968. In this way we hope to attract tax-deductible donations for the construction of the school buildings, and for further development. At the time of this writing, the legalities are in the process of being worked out. I hope that the generous reader, if he likes our educational ideas well enough to want to help further them, will bear us in mind for possible contributions.

Another plan for the near future is evolving from the fact that a growing number of our members are coming to feel attracted to the monastic ideal. It has long, in fact, been my belief that a monastic group functioning within the broader framework of a cooperative community would help immeasurably to strengthen the overall sense of spiritual purpose. *Sadhus,* or holy men, that live permanently in proximity to an Indian village are accounted a blessing on the whole community. Their renunciation inspires householders to cling less firmly to the thought of "me and mine."

My reason for starting a secular community first was not only because this is a special need of our times (there are numerous monasteries already in existence), but also because I felt, if I were going to start a secular community at all, that it would be unwise to try to develop it out of a monastic order. Inharmony would almost certainly result, even as it would in the life of an individual if he abandoned a completely dedicated for a more self-centered way of life. The monks would see in the lives of the more recently arrived householders a betrayal of their selfless principles. The householders would resent the monks for what they considered their narrow-mindedness. The monks, in setting the tone for the whole community, would seek to impose an unreasonable strictness on everyone. And the householders if they were not cowed into becoming mere sheep in their obedience (forgive the mixed metaphor; I couldn't resist it!), would probably set themselves in a determined attitude of rebellion. This, at least, is a pattern that I have had some opportunity to observe over the years.

The natural line of evolution is from the lower to the higher: in this case, from the secular to the spiritual. In India, where this fact is understood, there is rarely any friction between householders and monks, for it is felt that the latter are a blessing on the established order, rather than the householders being a misfortune to it.

Thus it was that I wanted to found Ananda first as a secular community. Now, however, that it has been founded and is flourishing, the time has arrived for us to add to our existing structure a monastic order. We have called this new order "The Friends of God." It has started with ten Ananda members: seven men and three women.

We have not set an absolute limit for the number of residents at Ananda, but I think a fair estimate would be about two hundred persons, including children. Of this number, not more than forty persons would live at the Retreat. Even two hundred residents would probably exceed our actual needs as a community, but it would permit the training of groups to send elsewhere for the formation of new communities.

Yes, we do plan to start other communities elsewhere. But as I have recommended in this book, each community will be autonomous; in this sense, it will not be a branch of Ananda, but an equal member of a kind of loose-knit fraternity.

As for our sense of responsibility to the cooperative community movement as a whole, it is in no way our desire to "make the scene." Our interests are practical. People who want to involve us in lengthy discussions on "theories" of communal living usually find that our answers are circumscribed by the expression, "Well, this is what we have found works." That, essentially, is the approach of this book: not the spinning of merely beautiful, but of *workable,* ideas.

Chapter Nine
"HERE AND NOW"

It is Tuesday, July 13, 1971, as I write these lines. (In 2013, however, I am polishing the work once more.) The day has been pleasantly warm, not hot; the sky has remained all day without a cloud. I lay in a Mexican hammock for awhile before returning to write this last chapter, and gazed peacefully across a wide valley at the High Sierra in the distance. Fading patches of snow still cling, as if pleading for protection, to the higher slopes. I imagined myself for a moment back in the Himalayas. And then I smiled. Why be anywhere in the world but right here, right now? Philosophically speaking, of course, that is always a good thought; but it is one that comes particularly naturally here at Ananda.

For months now I have enjoyed the seclusion I sought so longingly nine years ago. Will you say that it has taken me long enough to find it? But what are nine years? I consider that part of my life well spent. These have been years of inner growth as well as, perhaps, of some outward usefulness.

Life drifts by so quickly, almost unnoticeably, like a cloud. I know that this seclusion I now enjoy will not last indefinitely. Life itself will not last. I pray that, when my time comes to leave this world, it will be with a mental sky quite as empty of any clouds of attachment or desire as the sky above me has been this day. For what kind of home can we build here on earth? Ananda will flourish for a time. When it has fulfilled its purpose, it will go. To desire perfection in the outer world is a delusion. Only as a place for making great *inner* strides can Ananda fulfill its true purpose.

The time is 5:45 p.m. Residents and retreatants have just finished practicing energization exercises and yoga postures together on the deck outside the temple, about 150 feet from my house. A few moments ago I heard their footsteps as they entered the temple for meditation before supper. Later this evening they will gather again, to chant, meditate, offer healing prayers for others, and listen to a reading from one of the writings of our great Guru, Paramhansa Yogananda.

Every now and then the sound of a distant truck, or of an airplane overhead, breaks in upon the silence to remind us that that other world still exists "out there." More often what one hears is a bird singing, a lizard scurrying up a tree trunk, a bee in flight pausing briefly at a blossom.

A typical day at Ananda Meditation Retreat begins at six o'clock with exercise and meditation. No one is obliged to attend. Group activities are offered as a benefit, not as a rule, of membership. A few of our people prefer to meditate on their own. Breakfast, except on weekends, is at eight o'clock. There is another meditation at noon.

Soon after breakfast, work begins. Some of our residents

work here on the Retreat grounds. Others go to the Farm to work, whether at farming, or in one of our various industries. Ananda members make incense, health candy bars, artistic jewelry, pottery, clothing. They print books (including this one). They paint. They weave. They build geodesic domes. Anyone with a skill of his own is encouraged to put it to use. Ananda products are becoming increasingly popular in stores throughout California. Perhaps you have seen them?

Financially, at last, we are holding our own.

Life at the Farm is more hectic than at the Retreat. But hectic is a relative word. You go into the incense factory. The workers, some of them softly singing a devotional chant, look up and smile. As likely as not no words are exchanged; smiles are more eloquent.

Some of our members have asked me to give them Indian names. Jyotish, who founded the incense business a year and a half ago, functions informally also as the community's general manager. Capable, perceptive, marvelously patient—I think a large measure of our success is due to him.

And then I think how fortunate we are in this other person, and in that, and before I know it the list has grown too long for me to maintain a sharp focus on anyone. What makes us truly fortunate, I reflect, is that in this lifetime so many have been drawn to seek and to serve God.

Sonia, who held an important job in the city, and helped me substantially during my financial crisis in 1968, works now as our treasurer and general office manager. Her happy smile is a blessing on the community.

Haanel, our head farmer, is probably also our most erudite member. An elderly man with a delightful insight into the vagaries of life, he has been a famous photographer, and a hermit in Chilean jungles, as well as farming his own land in Vista, California. He came here two years ago. It is because of his expertise that we now have a flourishing farm.

Satya came here three years ago; he has been in charge of the Retreat ever since. Thanks to his steadfastness, the scheduled activities here flow smoothly the year around.

Most of our adults are in their twenties or early thirties. About seventy people, including children, presently live at the two places. But the number is growing. Even now at the Retreat there are several guests who hope to become permanent members.

Requirements for membership are that one be a disciple, or at least a sincere devotee, of our Guru, Paramhansa Yogananda, and of his line of Gurus, and that one have studied, or be in the process of studying, the yoga correspondence course from Ananda; that one be definitely and completely off of hallucinogenic drugs and alcoholic beverages; that one be able to pay his membership fee ($1,000 for single persons, $1,500 for married couples) upon acceptance, and be able in addition to pay for the construction of his own residence; that there be gainful employment for him in the community; and above all, that the community members feel an attunement with him and accept him.

After two years, we are finally on the verge of incorporating Ananda as a cooperative society. Our experience heretofore was inadequate to permit us to take this step. In some ways we regret having to take it now, but we know that it is necessary. Other formalities will probably become necessary also, as we grow. One reason we don't want to grow too large is so that we may keep our way of life as simple and as free of formalities as possible.

But life is a procession of seasons. New residents here often fear the approach of winter, but in the midst of it many of them find it even more beautiful than the summer months. So can life's changes be, if we accept them with inner peace.

This morning I had to break my silence to make a necessary phone call at the Farm. Upon returning, I noticed Satya sitting in the office, smiling, and looking particularly at peace with himself.

"You look happy," I said.

"How could one feel otherwise," he asked, "living here?"

AFTERWORD

June 1979.

Eight years have passed since those last lines were written; twelve years since I bought the first land at Ananda. The reader must wonder: How well have the ideas outlined here withstood the test of time?

Remarkably well, I am happy to say—not because we've bent objective realities to fit preconceived theories, but because most of these realities were anticipated in the theories. Ananda has grown organically, in creative response to tests and opportunities. Rarely, if ever, have we had to go back and restudy this book to see how we *ought* to do something. Yet even we were surprised, when preparing this new edition for publication, to find how closely the realities of 1979 reflect the theories of 1968.

Someday I'd like to rewrite this book to include in every chapter an up-to-date report on how, specifically, we've applied—or, in some cases, adjusted—the points it proposes. But for now let it suffice to say that this little book has been tested and proved, not only here at Ananda, but far afield. Indeed, hundreds of new communities have been influenced by it. (It is pleasant to reflect that one reason for the growing success of the modern communitarian movement may be the increasing acceptance of the ideas here set forth. Indeed, commentators have noted a shift among successful communities toward my proposals.)

Ananda itself has become one of the best-known "New Age" communities in the world. It hasn't achieved its present degree of success without considerable struggle. Our obstacles have included a county-imposed building moratorium that lasted nearly five years; and a forest fire that, three years ago, destroyed twenty-one homes at the farm, and devastated 425 of our present 650 acres "There are no such things as obstacles," Paramhansa Yogananda used to say, "there are only opportunities!" We have turned our obstacles into opportunities for greater growth spiritually, as well as materially. Ananda today can look back with pride on how far we've come, and forward with eager expectation of a shining new era of development.

At present our membership stands at approximately 180 permanent residents, and a large number of affiliated and non-resident members. New people are arriving in increasing numbers, particularly now that I have finished with writing for the time being, and have taken to touring the country, lecturing and teaching. My last and major work, *The Path: Autobiography of a Western Yogi*, was completed in 1977. Since January 1978, my life has changed dramatically, with many months spent outside Ananda. The community, too, reflecting this more out-going energy, has begun to carry its message outward through tours by several of our teachers, and through the establishment of a network of centers across the country.

Ananda now presents many of the features of a well-established village: a thriving farm, dairy, and apiary; various businesses, privately as well as community-owned; "how-to-live" schools for children from nursery school through high school; an apprentice program for nonmembers wishing to learn skills in a cooperative community setting; a market that sells our own produce; a car repair shop; a fledgling restaurant; a publications building and print shop; a construction company that has the reputation for building the finest homes in Nevada County; a cabinet shop; handcrafted goods; music lessons; and our own singing group, the Gandharvas (meaning Celestial Musicians). The list could be extended to considerable length. We have, for instance, a monastery called Ayodhya, home to about thirty-five monks and nuns. We have a successful health food store, called Earth Song, in Nevada City, and a just-starting craft shop named Mountain Song. We also have a new radio program, "Pathways to Superconsciousness," five days a week in San Francisco, and another program weekly in Nevada City. But if I tried to say it all I'd only overburden the reader. The purpose of this Afterword is rather to reassure him—you—that the plan *is* working. In fact, it is thriving.

What is thriving most of all is the spirit of joy that is implicit in our very name, Ananda. Ananda residents are famous for their cheerful, inwardly centered attitude, their openness and relative freedom from psychological defenses. Even the fire served only to affirm these attitudes. While John Novak (Jyotish), our general manager, watched the collapse of his home in which his wife, Devi, had given birth just ten days previously to their first child, he exclaimed, "Well, at least that solves the problem we were having with leaks!" As soon as the ground cooled sufficiently to walk on it, the members pitched in joyfully to clear away the charred remains and rebuild, this time better than ever. The county supervisors set aside the moratorium in this case, allowing us to build again the homes we'd lost. What we have now is nicer homes, views that we never knew we had, a park instead of a wilderness, with wide stretches of grass between tall trees, and a stronger spirit of dedication than ever before. Truly, "There are no such things as obstacles; there are only opportunities!" In the spirit here, far more than in our outward, material developments, the practical value of this book is being demonstrated. For what I have stressed throughout is the need primarily for *inner* change.

Our plans for the future include a natural healing school and clinic; an institute of cooperative spiritual living; a new and larger retreat (keeping the old one more strictly for seclusion and meditation); a network of "how-to-live" schools across the country, and an Ananda training program for school teachers; a ministerial training program; an annual "Festival of the Joyful Arts"; a music conservatory; a department of sciences dedicated to exploring new and simplified solutions to the problem of energy, and a more humanity-oriented technology; and a department for researching solutions that have been found by earlier, now vanishing, societies around the world.

If you'd like to know more about Ananda, please write, or

come visit us. Ananda Retreat is open the year around.

Our hope, finally, is not necessarily that everyone will join Ananda, or form other communities elsewhere, but that the ideals exemplified by such communities will spread out into society at large, inspiring people everywhere to live more co-operatively with one another and with nature, more open to spiritual values, and more centered and joyful in themselves.

SECOND AFTERWORD

It is now April 2013. I am visiting our community near Assisi, Italy (one of our ten communities worldwide, which have a total residency of about a thousand people). In June I will return to Ananda Village, Nevada City, for three months. Three months later I'll return to our work in India. I will soon be eighty-seven—old enough, perhaps, to "call it a day." But things keep happening. This fall a film will be released worldwide about Ananda, called *Finding Happiness*. Eight more films are planned, though I will need to be personally involved in only some of them. I have one more book to write: *The Promise of Immortality, Part II*. Perhaps I'll get an opportunity for a little of that seclusion that has been my lifelong dream.

It may be fairly said that I've done a fair amount in my life: started nine communities; written 150 books; composed about 420 songs and instrumental pieces; taken some 15,000 art color slides; given countless thousands of lectures and classes in many countries, and in five languages.

Ananda has now become more than a place: It is a principle. Our communities have shown that it is possible to live in brotherhood, harmony, and serviceful happiness.

All that I have done has been for God and for my Guru. I

have had no personal desire in anything that has been accomplished.

Many years ago, Daya Mata[8] said to me, "I look forward to the day when I can look back and see what a great work Master has accomplished in coming to this world."

I answered her. "By then, I hope I really won't care. This is all God's dream, not my own. I will be happy to have been of service to it, but in the end, that's all it is: a dream. God is the only reality."

---

8 Daya Mata (1914–2010) was the second president, after Yogananda's passing, of Self-Realization Fellowship. —ed.

About the Author

"Swami Kriyananda is a man of wisdom and compassion in action, truly one of the leading lights in the spiritual world today."

—Lama Surya Das, Dzogchen Center, author of *Awakening the Buddha Within*

A prolific author, accomplished composer, playwright, and artist, and a world-renowned spiritual teacher, Swami Kriyananda (1926—2013) referred to himself simply as "a humble disciple" of the great God-realized master, Paramhansa Yogananda. He met his guru at the young age of twenty-two, and served him during the last four years of the master's life. He dedicated the rest of his life to sharing Yogananda's teachings throughout the world.

Kriyananda was born in Romania of American parents, and educated in Europe, England, and the United States. Philosophically and artistically inclined from youth, he soon came to question life's meaning and society's values. During a period of intense inward reflection, he discovered Yogananda's *Autobiography of a Yogi*, and immediately traveled three thousand miles from New York to California to meet the master, who accepted him as a monastic disciple. Yogananda appointed him as the head of the monastery, authorized him to teach in his name and to give initiation into Kriya Yoga, and entrusted him with the missions of writing and developing what he called "world-brotherhood colonies."

Recognized as the "father of the spiritual communities movement" in the United States, Swami Kriyananda founded the Ananda World Brotherhood Community in the Sierra Nevada Foothills of Northern California in 1968. It has served as a model for nine communities founded subsequently in the United States, Europe, and India.

Dear Reader,

Ananda is a worldwide work based on the same teachings expressed in this book—those of the great spiritual teacher, Paramhansa Yogananda. If you enjoyed this title, Crystal Clarity Publishers invites you to continue to deepen your spiritual life through the many avenues of Ananda Worldwide—including meditation communities, centers, and groups; online virtual community and webinars; retreat centers offering classes and teacher training in yoga and meditation; and more.

For special offers and discounts for first-time visitors to Ananda, visit:

http://www.crystalclarity.com/welcome

Feel free to contact us. We are here to serve you.

Joy to you,

Crystal Clarity Publishers

ANANDA WORLDWIDE

Ananda, a worldwide organization founded by Swami Kriyananda, offers spiritual support and resources based on the teachings of Paramhansa Yogananda. There are Ananda spiritual communities in Nevada City, Sacramento, and Palo Alto, California; Seattle, Washington; Portland and Laurelwood, Oregon; as well as a retreat center and European community in Assisi, Italy, and a community near New Delhi, India. Ananda supports more than 140 meditation groups worldwide.

For more information about Ananda's work, our communities, or meditation groups near you, please call 530.478.7560 or visit www.ananda.org.

THE EXPANDING LIGHT

The Expanding Light is the largest retreat center in the world to share exclusively the teachings of Paramhansa Yogananda. Situated in the Ananda Village community, it offers the opportunity to experience spiritual life in a contemporary ashram setting. The varied, year-round schedule of classes and programs on yoga, meditation, and spiritual practice includes Karma Yoga, Personal Retreat, Spiritual Travel, and online learning. The Ananda School of Yoga & Meditation offers certified yoga, yoga therapist, spiritual counselor, and meditation teacher trainings. Large groups are welcome.

The teaching staff are experts in Kriya Yoga meditation and all aspects of Yogananda's teachings. All staff members live at Ananda Village and bring an uplifting approach to their areas of service. The serene natural setting and delicious vegetarian meals help provide an ideal environment for a truly meaningful visit.

For more information, please call 800.346.5350
or visit www.expandinglight.org.

CRYSTAL CLARITY PUBLISHERS

Crystal Clarity Publishers offers many additional resources to assist you in your spiritual journey, including many other books (see the following pages for some of them), a wide variety of inspirational and relaxation music composed by Swami Kriyananda, and yoga and meditation videos. To request a catalog, place an order for the above products, or to find out more information, please contact us at:

Crystal Clarity Publishers / www.crystalclarity.com
14618 Tyler Foote Rd. / Nevada City, CA 95959
TOLL FREE: 800.424.1055 or 530.478.7600
FAX: 530.478.7610
EMAIL: clarity@crystalclarity.com

For our online catalog, complete with secure ordering, please visit our website.

Further Explorations _____

AUTOBIOGRAPHY OF A YOGI
Paramhansa Yogananda

Autobiography of a Yogi is one of the best-selling Eastern philosophy titles of all time, with millions of copies sold, named one of the best and most influential books of the twentieth century. This highly prized reprinting of the original 1946 edition is the only one available free from textual changes made after Yogananda's death. Yogananda was the first yoga master of India whose mission was to live and teach in the West.

In this updated edition are bonus materials, including a last chapter that Yogananda wrote in 1951, without posthumous changes. This new edition also includes the eulogy that Yogananda wrote for Gandhi, and a new foreword and afterword by Swami Kriyananda, one of Yogananda's close, direct disciples.

Also available in unabridged audiobook (MP3) format, read by Swami Kriyananda.

PARAMHANSA YOGANANDA
A Biography with Personal Reflections and Reminiscences
Swami Kriyananda

Paramhansa Yogananda's classic *Autobiography of a Yogi* is more about the saints Yogananda met than about himself—in spite of Yogananda's astonishing accomplishments.

Now, one of Yogananda's direct disciples relates the untold story of this great spiritual master and world teacher: his teenage miracles, his challenges in coming to America, his national lecture campaigns, his struggles to fulfill his world-changing mission amid incomprehension and painful betrayals, and his ultimate triumphant achievement. Kriyananda's subtle grasp of his guru's inner nature reveals Yogananda's many-sided greatness. Includes many never-before-published anecdotes.

Also available in unabridged audiobook (MP3) format, read by Swami Kriyananda.

THE NEW PATH
My Life with Paramhansa Yogananda
Swami Kriyananda

When Swami Kriyananda discovered *Autobiography of a Yogi* in 1948, he was totally new to Eastern teachings. This is a great advantage to the Western reader, since Kriyananda walks us along the yogic path as he discovers it from the moment of his initiation as a disciple of Yogananda. With winning honesty, humor, and deep insight, he shares his journey on the spiritual path through personal stories and experiences.

Through more than four hundred stories of life with Yogananda, we tune in more deeply to this great master and to the teachings he brought to the West. This book is an ideal complement to *Autobiography of a Yogi*.

More Books from Crystal Clarity Publishers

The Essence of the Bhagavad Gita
Explained by Paramhansa Yogananda
As Remembered by his disciple, Swami Kriyananda

Demystifying Patanjali
The Wisdom of Paramhansa Yogananda Presented by his direct disciple, Swami Kriyananda

The Essence of Self-Realization
The Wisdom of Paramhansa Yogananda Recorded, Compiled, and Edited by his disciple, Swami Kriyananda

Conversations with Yogananda
Recorded, with Reflections, by his disciple, Swami Kriyananda

Revelations of Christ
Proclaimed by Paramhansa Yogananda Presented by his disciple, Swami Kriyananda

Whispers from Eternity
Paramhansa Yogananda
Edited by his disciple, Swami Kriyananda

The Rubaiyat of Omar Khayyam
Paramhansa Yogananda
Edited by his disciple, Swami Kriyananda

–The Wisdom of Yogananda series–
How To Be Happy All the Time
Karma and Reincarnation
Spiritual Relationships
How To Be a Success
How To Have Courage, Calmness, and Confidence
How To Achieve Glowing Health and Vitality

Meditation for Starters with CD
Swami Kriyananda

Intuition for Starters
Swami Kriyananda

Chakras for Starters
Savitri Simpson

Vegetarian Cooking for Starters
Diksha McCord

The Art and Science of Raja Yoga
Swami Kriyananda

Awaken to Superconsciousness
Swami Kriyananda

Living Wisely, Living Well
Swami Kriyananda

The Bhagavad Gita
According to Paramhansa Yogananda
Edited by his disciple, Swami Kriyananda

How to Meditate
Jyotish Novak

Self-Expansion Through Marriage
Swami Kriyananda

The Time Tunnel
Swami Kriyananda

The Yugas
Joseph Selbie & David Steinmetz

God Is for Everyone
Inspired by Paramhansa Yogananda As taught to and understood by his disciple, Swami Kriyananda

Religion in the New Age
Swami Kriyananda

The Art of Supportive Leadership
J. Donald Walters (Swami Kriyananda)

Money Magnetism
J. Donald Walters (Swami Kriyananda)

Two Souls: Four Lives
Catherine Kairavi

In Divine Friendship
Swami Kriyananda

30-Day Essentials for Marriage
Jyotish Novak

30-Day Essentials for Career
Jyotish Novak

Education for Life
J. Donald Walters (Swami Kriyananda)

The Peace Treaty
J. Donald Walters (Swami Kriyananda)

Pilgrimage to Guadalupe
Swami Kriyananda

Love Perfected, Life Divine
Swami Kriyananda